THE PATH TO
CHRISTLIKENESS

Tom Payne

Essential Growth Solutions, LLC
Chicago, Illinois

THE PATH TO CHRISTLIKENESS

ISBN-13: 978-0999507421

ISBN-10: 0999507427

For additional information about Tom Payne and his books please visit www.tompayne.com.

Published by:

Essential Growth Solutions, LLC

Chicago, Illinois

To the memory of Watchman Nee

CONTENTS

INTRODUCTION: RESTLESSNESS

THE HUMAN CONDITION

There is an emptiness at the center of our souls and it will not let us rest until we fill it. It launches us on a lifelong quest for satiation and this pursuit expresses itself in many ways. Some people chase after fame, others struggle to amass power, or possessions and riches. These worldly paths can provide momentary satisfaction, but ultimately the hunger returns. The void in our souls demands more, always more, and we restlessly respond. But no matter how much we partake of the world's empty calories, they fail to satisfy us.

Perhaps the worst symptom generated by this emptiness is the way it is so self-centering. We are like starving men and women whose thoughts can only focus on our empty bellies. Additionally, this self-centered nature desires glory. We want to finish first, occupy the top of the org chart, receive the awards, make more money and possess nicer things than our "neighbors." We like to sit in an airplane's first-class seats so we can watch the proles schlep by. But once we arrive at our intended destination, wherever it is, we discover the emptiness is still with us, sending us down yet another blind alley that ends in ravenous hunger.

We find this meaningless, worldly life in Ecclesiastes where its author, the Preacher, built gardens, parks, buildings and pools for his enjoyment. He accumulated flocks, herds, silver, gold and many concubines. He pursued wisdom and drank wine. He also boasted, "So I became great, and surpassed all who were before me in Jerusalem" (Ec 2:9). Yet he eventually realized that his self-centered, self-exalting life that enabled him to surpass everyone, "was vanity and a striving after wind" (Ec 2:11).

Some people are able to see how the world's paths are dead ends, and this inspires them to follow a religion to find peace. Yet virtually every "spiritual" answer leads us astray. The only exception is the Way that is

Christ. It is the only Path that fills the void inside of us, enabling us to rest.

This idea of spiritual exclusivity infuriates the modern mind which believes inclusivity should be one of the Ten Commandments. But once we compare the world's religions to the Path, we can see why it is the only Way, for it is the only religion that treats our self-centering disease.

THE MAN-MADE PATHS

Other than Christianity, every religion is based on "scriptures" written by someone whose vision was warped by the self-centering nature we all share. The proof of this is found in the religions they created. "Self" is the answer in their religious systems. If you seek salvation, then your actions will save you. You are your own savior. It is a different type of self-exaltation from the world's paths, but it is self-exaltation nonetheless.

Let's take a brief look at the world's three largest religions, apart from the largest faith, which is Christianity, and answer the question, "Are they paths wherein the individual is his own savior?"

For Buddha, the universal malady was suffering. He then developed a religious course of therapy to liberate us from suffering and it is called the Noble Eightfold Path. It involved: Right view, right intention, right speech, right action, right livelihood, right effort, right mindfulness, and right concentration. On this path I am the one making the right effort, practicing right mindfulness and right concentration, etc.

In other words, salvation, or enlightenment, does not come from God, but from my actions. And in the earliest forms of Buddhism there was no mention of God. No God, only self... if ever there was a self-centering, self-exalting faith, then Buddhism is it.

In Hinduism, dharma, or right living, is considered to be the same thing as truth itself, and right living is the highest attainment of a human being. The idea of karma is one wherein our good or bad actions generate merits or demerits. Your fate is determined by how you live. You are the author of your destiny, the savior of your own soul.

In Islam one's spiritual destiny is also determined by how you live and what you do. We read this from the website www.islamreligion.com:

> Islam teaches us that salvation is attainable through the worship of God alone. A person must believe in God and follow His commandments.
>
> ...In addition to this Islam teaches us that human beings are born without sin and are naturally inclined to worship God alone (without any intermediaries). To retain this state of sinlessness humankind must only follow God's commandments and *strive to live a righteous life.* [My note: Emphasis added.]

It could not be clearer. You, who "strive to live a righteous life," are the author of your own salvation in Islam.

If we have a dis-eased soul whose symptoms are being self-centered and prone to self-exaltation, then can you imagine the following prescription: Focus on the actions of the self (self-centered), for they will save you (self-exaltation). Wouldn't this prescription feed the disease?

THE REVEALED RELIGION

The Path to Christlikeness, or the Christian faith, moves in the opposite direction of the other religions, because it opposes human nature. It is centered on God and others, and not self. In fact, self plays no role in our salvation on the Path. (More on that in the next chapter.) Therefore, the process of salvation in Christianity does not reinforce the self-centered, self-exalting nature of our souls.

No self-centered person could have created this other-centered faith. So, God revealed His Way to us through His Son, and His Spirit-anointed prophets and apostles. The Apostle Paul wrote about how the Christian faith he shared with us was not something he invented, or was taught; God revealed it to him:

> For I would have you know, brothers, that the gospel that was preached by me is not man's gospel. For I did not receive it from any man, nor was I taught it, but I received it through a revelation of Jesus Christ (Gal 1:11-12).

Since God is love, and the Path is based on God's other-centered nature and not our own, it has this unique feature: It can be extremely difficult to navigate. Our nature shouts, "Go left!" Meanwhile, the Path moves sharply right. Many great saints felt lost on the Path while they were making their greatest progress. As Martin Luther summarized:

> Samson, David, and many other excellent men, fell into grievous sins. Job and Jeremiah cursed the day of their birth. Elijah and Jonah became weary of life and prayed for death. Such offenses on the part of the saints, the Scriptures record for the comfort of those who are near despair. No person has ever sunk so low that he cannot rise again. On the other hand, no man's standing is so secure that he may not fall.[1]

God designed a Path that is beyond our comprehension because His ways are not ours:

---

[1] Martin Luther, *Commentary on the Epistle to the Galatians*. Transl. Theodore Graebner, (Grand Rapids, MI: Christian Classics Ethereal Library, 1538), p. 36.

> For my thoughts are not your thoughts,
> *neither are your ways my ways*, declares the LORD.
> For as the heavens are higher than the earth,
> *so are my ways higher than your ways*
> and my thoughts than your thoughts (Is 55:8-9, emphasis added).

We are unable to understand God's "ways," or His thoughts, on our own. But the Spirit of God understands them, and Jesus promised us that the Holy Spirit would guide us "into all the truth" (Jn 16:13). Understanding God's "ways" is vital to our journey if we are to walk on the Path in peace, confident in God's love even as He leads us into dark, painful places, as He did with Job, Elijah, Jonah and others.

If the Path is a spiritual course of treatment that is designed to heal us—and it is—then to understand it better we need to understand our disease. The nature of our illness first appeared in a story known as the Fall of Adam and Eve.

THE FALL

Adam and Eve's story begins with God creating them in His image. Since Christ "is the image of God" (Col 1:15), our ancient ancestors were originally Christlike in Paradise. To remain image bearers of God, Adam and Eve needed to obey one, simple command: Do not eat the fruit from the tree of the knowledge of good and evil. For if you do, you will die.

At first, there was Adam, Eve and God in Paradise, but a fourth character entered the play. It was the "ancient serpent, who is called the devil and Satan, the deceiver of the whole world" (Rev 12:9). True to his deceptive character, the serpent lied to Eve by telling her she would not die if she ate the forbidden fruit. "The deceiver of the whole world" was making God out to be a liar! And then he added this tempting, self-exalting promise: She would "be like God" (Gen 3:5).

In a very limited sense, what Satan said was true. When Eve ate the forbidden fruit, she became God-like in that she shared God's ability to know good and evil. But she became the exact opposite of God in every other way. For God is life, and she became spiritually dead. God is holy, and she became tainted with sin. The image of God is Christ but, once she ate this fruit, she began to reflect the image of the serpent; for like the serpent, she became a rebel against God's will.

Eve's faith was being tested in the Garden of Eden. Who would she believe, God or Satan? Whose desires would she choose to satisfy? Would it be God's desire for her, or what was becoming her own desire to become like God through disobedience?

As the tendrils of Satan's temptation began to enter and encircle Eve's soul, she began to see the world around her in a new light. For example, she saw "that the tree was good for food," (Gen 3:6). But in reality, it was the deadliest of poisons, and there was no antidote yet available.

Eve was seeing the opposite of reality. Her world was being turned upside-down. The forbidden tree, and its deadly fruit, was now "a delight to the eyes, and … was to be desired to make one wise" (Gen 3:6). You will be like God! You will be wise! She was infected by the self-centering, self-exalting poison of Satan's temptation.

Eve was now spiritually blinded by her fledgling faith in Satan and his false promises. She acted on this bad faith and ate the fruit. Now she knew good and evil, and it revealed to her the enormity of her sin. She felt exposed, naked and ashamed, and could see how the serpent, not God, had deceived her.

Adam stood by Eve's side as she violated God's command. Then he joined Eve in her sin by also eating the forbidden fruit. For their sin, Adam and Eve fell from grace and were expelled from Paradise.

THE FALL'S EFFECTS

Theologians have noted the self-centering effects of the Fall and sin. Jonathan Edwards described the impact of the Fall as follows:

> The ruin that the fall brought upon the soul of man consists very much in his losing the nobler and more benevolent principles of his nature, and falling wholly under the power and government of self-love.
> …Sin, like some powerful astringent, contracted his soul to the very small dimensions of selfishness; and God was forsaken, and fellow creatures forsaken, and man retired within himself and became totally governed by narrow and selfish principles and feelings. Self-love became absolute master of his soul, and the more noble and spiritual principles of his being took wing and flew away.[2]

Martin "Luther described the man in sin as incurvatus in se (bent inward upon himself) whereas the man in Christ looks away from himself toward God and his neighbor in love."[3]

The picture taking shape is of a human race wherein everyone is the spiritual equivalent of a black hole, a star that collapses inward upon itself

---

[2] Jonathan Edwards, *Charity and Its Fruits; or Christian Love as Manifested in the Heart and Life* (NY: Robert Carter and Brothers, 1856), pp. 226-227, 227-228.

[3] Donald G. Bloesch, *Essentials of Evangelical Theology, Volume One: God, Authority and Salvation* (Peabody, MA: Prince Press, 1978), p. 92.

and creates such a powerful gravitational pull that nothing can escape it, not even light. We were created to radiate light one day, but after the Fall our misshapen souls could not even let light escape. Men and women, the images of God, became images of complete spiritual ruin.

The focus of a fallen soul, no matter how hard we try to make it otherwise, is our self. Even our attempts to love others, serve others, do unto others, is colored by a soul that always calculates, consciously or subconsciously, how the effort will enrich himself. This corrupts all that we do, including the creation of religions. Therefore, the man-made religions are self-centric when it comes to matters of salvation, but in the one "revealed" religion, salvation is based on what our Savior-God does.

A PATH UNLIKE ANY OTHER

Now that we are acquainted with how our souls are deformed by sin, it is easier to understand the Path and how it is different from every other. God's Path leads us in the opposite direction of our natural tendencies, because our natural tendencies lead us away from God. Our desire to be like God leads us to seek the sunlit mountain tops of glory. But the Path to Christlikeness will humble us, and sometimes lead us into the valley of the shadow of death where the sun's rays cannot reach.

We believe we must contribute to our salvation through various actions like prayer, fasting, good works, confession, meditation, pursuing wisdom, and building up knowledge. But the Path to Christlikeness tells us we are spiritually dead (Eph 2:5), just like our fallen forebears, Adam and Eve, and dead people cannot save themselves.

We believe if we live good lives, then we will be saved—the essence of the Hindu and Islamic faiths. But God tells us our righteous works "are like a polluted garment" (Is 64:6). For if our nature is soiled, then every "garment" we cover ourselves with becomes soiled.

We desire to be first, but the Path declares the first will be last, and the last will be first. We want to rule, but the Path tells us the greatest among us will be servants and slaves.

Note the constant inversion taking place on the Path. To make our upside-down world right-side-up, God must reverse the reversal. Sin stood us on our heads. Satan's influence warped our vision to the point where we now see the opposite of what is real. So, God reverses this inversion by lifting us up and putting us back on our feet. He then gives us His Word to believe in and follow. It is to be our guide on the Path: "Your word is a lamp to my feet and a light to my path" (Ps 119:105).

To see how God's reversal of Satan's inversion takes place, we return to the Garden of Eden. Eve sinned when she ate the forbidden fruit, and her sinful action was the result of bad faith. She did not believe God; she believed Satan.

To save fallen humanity, God devised a Path wherein faith—a saving belief in God's words, or His gospel—enables us to return to His presence and Paradise. Adam and Eve did not believe God's words in the Garden, but we can reverse the effects of the Fall by believing the good news. Instead of believing what our eyes see, we are to believe the Word of God.

The first message from Jesus' lips, in the Gospel according to Mark was, "repent and believe in the gospel" (Mk 1:15)." A fruit of conversion is repentance. Once saved our mind and purpose changes, and this is the definition of repentance. We are now moving in a different direction. Repentance is the essence of the divine inversion. We were going left, now we are going right. Our minds were centered on ourselves, and now our focus is shifting to God and others.

Faith is the foundation of a Christian's life and our ability to live a God-honoring life is in direct relation to the depth of our faith in Him. To develop a deeper faith, God continually tests it throughout our lives. This has always been so for the children of God, both those who looked forward to the coming of Christ and those who've lived after His ascension into the heavens.

ELIJAH'S FAITH IN GOD

Just as there are people who are considered "most likely to succeed," there are also prophets who are "most unlikely to fail a faith test." Elijah was such a prophet. His faith was fortified by witnessing the power of God on several occasions. A dramatic example of this was when he challenged the 450 prophets of Baal, and the 400 prophets of Asherah, to put their god to a test. Would their god be able to consume a burnt offering?

Elijah believed his God would pass this test, for he told them "…and the God who answers by fire, he is God" (1 Ki 18:24).

Their god did nothing, and Elijah, one prophet against 850 false prophets, mocked them and their god. (His haughty, sarcastic tone may have been the symptom of a pride infection. More on this in a moment.) He then called upon the LORD and fire came down from heaven to consume his burnt offering. After this dramatic display of God's power, he ordered the Israelites to capture and kill every one of these false prophets. These evil shepherds who led the Israelites down false paths had to be removed, and they were.

To confront so many men required great courage and faith. The spiritual position of Elijah, the mighty man of God, was certainly secure at this point in his walk with God. Or was it? I am reminded of Martin Luther's words, quoted above, "On the other hand, no man's standing is so secure that he may not fall." And those words applied to Elijah. He collapsed under the crushing weight of his prophetic burden.

ENTERING THE SUNLESS VALLEY

King Ahab's wife, Jezebel, who had these false prophets dine at her table, pronounced a death sentence on Elijah. Elijah had ordered the deaths of her spiritual advisors and friends, and she ordered his death in return. Elijah responded by fleeing into the wilderness and praying to God to take his life.

It was a stunning abdication of his prophetic responsibilities. What happened to his faith in God? It was being tested and Elijah was failing this test. He appeared lost and confused on God's perplexing Path.

Was Elijah's turning away from his prophetic calling permanent? Was his fall from grace irreversible?

No. This moment of weakness did not disqualify Elijah from receiving the Lord's blessing. His failing the faith-test, of trusting God as his life was being threatened, did not result in him being banished from the presence of God. Quite the opposite. A short time later, while transferring his ministry to Elisha, he was swept up into the heavens on a chariot of fire to be with the Lord forever. Later on, Elijah and Moses, would meet with Jesus on the Mount of Transfiguration in glorified bodies. Few people in history have ever been as honored as Elijah.

So, how do these spiritual honors make sense? Is our failure to live up to our faith what is truly blessed?

GRACE REQUIRES A HUMBLE HEART

Though the Bible does not explicitly tell us this, Elijah's pride, as he was being used mightily by God, must have grown to a spiritually dangerous level. It is human for this to happen, and it happened to the Apostle Paul.

Paul was caught up to paradise and received revelations from God that were so profound he was not allowed to share them. The experience overwhelmed his senses. He did not know if he was in his body or out of it during these revelations. Such favor, even though it was from the hand of God, might make Paul prideful. But Christ had a plan to protect Paul from this spiritually-incapacitating sin.

Paul wrote, "So *to keep me from becoming conceited* because of the surpassing greatness of the revelations, a thorn was given me in the flesh, a messenger of Satan to harass me, *to keep me from becoming conceited*" (2 Cor 12:7, emphasis added).

Paul's fallen nature, like our own, was inclined toward pride. Pride commits two sins simultaneously. It exalts self and it looks down on others. It makes us deaf to the Word of God. When the proud heart hears, "the first shall be last," it laughs at such nonsense.

To treat our self-exalting sin-nature, God "opposes the proud but gives grace to the humble" (1 Pt 5:5). The reason why the last shall be first, is because God extends His spiritual blessings and power—His grace—to those who have been humbled, or made last. This humbling can take place in the lives of individuals like Elijah, but also in the collective lives of nations, and to the citizens of the entire world, as the Covid-19 pandemic revealed.

THE PATH DURING PLAGUE YEARS

God's refining fire grows hotter during plague years, like the ones we experienced during the Covid pandemic. This time of stomach-churning turbulence tested our faith. People were stressed, exhausted and wanted to check out. Several people, who are believers in Christ, told me, "I can't take it anymore." They'd reached the point of capitulation. The certainty and peace of mind they sought was overwhelmed by the chaos and confusion of a world gone mad.

What happened to them? Where was their rest in Christ?

As we anxiously look at the upheaval shaking the world, and feel a suffocating fear slowly spreading over us, we can never rest. We are living by sight, not faith, and our fear is an expression of our disbelief. We need to believe God's words. The Word of God tells us, "Trust not what you see. Trust the Word of God that tells you, 'God is in control.' "

We are back in Eden, where the serpent's strategy was to get Adam and Eve to doubt God's words. When our forebears doubted God, and believed what the serpent told them, they were exiled from Paradise. Today it is the sowers of chaos who are trying to shake our faith. Though we might occasionally hold Adam and Eve in contempt for their sin that led to the Fall, we commit their sin when we fail to believe God's words.

Our faith needs to be strengthened to meet the spiritual needs of this hour. And as we stumble, fall, cry, scream at God, and even wallow in self-pity, many of us will fail to see how God is accomplishing His purpose in our lives. He is humbling us and turning us away from independence and toward God-dependence.

If we are to maintain our belief in God's love, and completely trust Him during times of extreme faith-testing, then we need to understand the nature of the Path. For as we suffer under God's discipline—sometimes for years—it is easy to forget that He is operating on our hearts for our good.

God will strip away everything—if need be—from the children He loves until they understand that He is their portion and nothing more is needed. Another way of expressing this thought is, "If you have Jesus, you have everything." It sounds simplistic, almost childlike, but it is true.

A COURSE IN DISCIPLESHIP

To help us navigate this perplexing Path let us deepen our understanding of its times of anointing and times of testing. The seven feasts of Moses are like signposts that delineate the Path's many disorienting tests and periods of fruitfulness. They form our curriculum in the discipleship-training program of Jesus. The feasts have much to teach us about God's ways, and when we feel lost upon the Path, they can help reorient us and reinforce our trust in God our Savior.

"Moed" is the Hebrew word for "appointed feast," and it can also be translated as "appointed time." Each feast represents an appointed time in our lives during which we learn new lessons, and ultimately graduate to higher levels of spiritual maturity. So, think of these feasts, that appear in the table below, as steps toward becoming more Christlike.

The Stages	Order	Festival	Month	Day (s)
Stage One	1	Passover	1	14
	2	Unleavened Bread	1	15-21
	3	Firstfruits	1	16
Stage Two	4	Weeks, Pentecost, Harvest	3	6
Stage Three	5	Trumpets, Rosh Hashanah	7	1
	6	Day of Atonement, Yom Kippur	7	10
	7	Tabernacles, Ingathering, Booths	7	15-22

The first feast, Passover, marks the beginning of the Path that then continues with the remaining six feasts. We will study each of them in the chapters that follow and explore their rich, spiritual significance that we often overlook when reading the Bible.

This Path to Christlikeness is designed to treat our restless condition and restore the image of God that we were created in. We now start the most significant journey of our lives as we leave the spiritual re-birth canal and emerge as born-again children of God.

STAGE ONE:

FAITH

1

THE FEAST OF PASSOVER

THE STORY OF PASSOVER

Passover is the story about the Israelite's first-born children who were saved from death by the blood of a lamb. It is our story too, for Passover is an illustration of how we are saved, or spiritually reborn. For those unfamiliar with its story, I will briefly recount some of the highlights.

God visited ten plagues on the Egyptian people to get Pharaoh to release the Israelites from their enslavement. The final plague targeted and killed every first-born child in Egypt, including Pharaoh's eldest son and heir. The only first-born children who survived were those who dwelt in homes that had the blood of a defect-free sheep, or goat, marking its lintel and two doorposts. Then, when the "destroyer," an angel of death, saw this blood, he would *pass over* the people who dwelt safely inside. It did not matter if these people were saintly or wicked. The only thing that mattered was the presence of the right type of blood.

Once again, we are back in the Garden of Eden. God commanded the Israelites to do one thing, and if they failed to do it death would be the result. But the children of God obeyed this simple command, unlike Adam and Eve, and their first-born children escaped death. As we will see, there are two types of people in this world: Those who are facing eternal death, and those who are protected by the blood of a Lamb.

"OUR PASSOVER LAMB"

Prior to salvation, we are like the first-born in Egypt living in homes not marked by the blood of a lamb. But we are saved from this death sentence by believing the good news about God the Son, Jesus, and one way this "faith" has been defined is a "faith in his blood" (Rom 3:25). It is the

13

saving belief that Christ is our Lord who saved us from sin and death by dying for us, and paying the debt our sin incurred.

This sin-debt for us is the same as it was for Adam and Eve: Death. Whoever has sinned (and all have sinned) is under a sentence of death. Were it not for the crucifixion we would be condemned to die in our sins, and be alienated from God forever.

Jesus, our Lord and Savior, is the "defect-free," or sinless, "Lamb of God, who takes away the sin of the world" (Jn 1:29). And He takes away our sin by dying in our place. He is "our Passover lamb" (1 Cor 5:7), and His blood marks our dwelling forever.

We see this blood-salvation connection when the Bible states, "we have now been justified by his blood" (Rom 5:9). To be justified is to be saved. When we are justified, we are declared "not guilty" and "righteous" at the same time. The justified are judged to be in a right relationship with God, because their sin is washed away by the blood of the Lamb. After salvation we will sin, but the death penalty will always be averted by the invisible presence of His blood.

Passover is like a portal one goes through to move from death to life, and from the world's path to the Path to Christlikeness. On one side of the portal is the restless striving for the ephemeral, while on the other side is the embrace of the eternal that eventually bestows upon us the perfect peace of God.

GRACE AND FREEDOM

When you've lived your entire life as a slave, the transition to freedom can be difficult. For some, like the Israelites who were freed from bondage in Egypt, it was impossible. They not only grumbled against God about the privations of the wilderness, they actually sought to return to Egypt and slavery:

> "Would it not be better for us to go back to Egypt?" And they said to one another, "Let us choose a leader and go back to Egypt" (Num 14:3-4).

Though freed from Egypt they were still slaves, because they trusted in the provision of Pharaoh more than the provision of God. Faith in God is what liberates us, and a lack of faith enslaves us. After the Israelites saw God's mighty works liberate them, they were still unable to believe that God could secure the Promised Land for them. For when twelve men came back from the Promised Land, after spying it out for forty days, ten of them doubted they could take the land from the giants who dwelled therein. Their faith in the power of giants exceeded their faith in Almighty God. At every step in the wilderness, the Israelites revealed their bad faith.

God turned their forty days of spying into forty years of wandering in the wilderness until everyone, twenty years or older, died in this waste land. Caleb and Joshua, the two spies who trusted God's ability to give them the Promised Land, were the only exceptions. A new generation needed to be raised up, one capable of looking to God and trusting that His power was more than enough to make good on His promises.

Faith in God—specifically faith in Jesus, or God the Son—leads to freedom. Until we trust God, we are not free. We are slaves of the enemy of faith: Fear. We are paralyzed by the uncertainty of tomorrow and awed by the giants in our way. This cowardice toward God's enemies keeps us from effectively serving Him.

Courage is a by-product of faith in God, because when you believe God is with you, then who could possibly stand against you? And even if God's will is for you to lose your battle, according to the judgment of the world, your faith knows your sacrifice will be turned into a victory by God.

An illustration of a "defeat" in the world's eyes, but a victory in the eyes of God, is the martyrdom of the saints. In centuries past, they were offered a Christ-denying life or a faithful-to-the-end death. Their faith enabled them to conquer their fear of death and testify that Jesus is Lord. God anointed their sacrifice and made it spiritually powerful enough to open the eyes of many who were enslaved by Satan and his world system. Their blood was instrumental in overthrowing the Roman Empire. More on that in a moment.

SALVATION BY GRACE ALONE THROUGH FAITH ALONE

If Eve was blinded by just the temptation to sin—she saw "that the tree was good for food" before she ate the fruit—then how much more blinding is sin itself? Our fallen state makes the Way that is Christ impenetrably dark, and it is impossible for us to see and understand God's truth until we are born again.

Prior to being saved, I read the Bible often and I remembered many of its verses, but I understood none of it. The idea of being saved by simply trusting in Jesus, and accepting Him as my Lord and Savior, made no sense to me. Self-salvation was the only path that seemed reasonable to my fallen, rational mind. Martin Luther knew this roadblock to faith all too well. He wrote:

> The heart of man finds it difficult to believe that so great a treasure as the Holy Ghost is gotten by the mere hearing of faith. The hearer likes to reason like this: Forgiveness of sins, deliverance from death, the gift of the Holy Ghost, everlasting life are grand things. If you want to obtain these priceless benefits,

you must engage in correspondingly great efforts. And the devil says, "Amen."[1]

What removed the blindfold from my eyes was the presentation of the gospel found in a slender paperback entitled, *Sit, Walk, Stand*. It was written by Watchman Nee, a Chinese Christian who was imprisoned for his faith after Mao Zedong and the communists came to power. Nee believed the cure for a person's "sin-sick soul" had nothing to do with what we did, and everything to do with what Christ did. He wrote:

> We constantly speak of being "saved through faith," but what do we mean by it? We mean this, that we are saved by reposing in the Lord Jesus. *We did nothing whatever to save ourselves*; we simply laid upon him the burden of our sin-sick souls. *We began our Christian life by depending not upon our own doing but upon what he had done.* Until a man does this, he is no Christian; for to say: "I can do nothing to save myself; but by his grace God has done everything for me in Christ," is to take the first step in the life of faith. The Christian life from start to finish is based upon this utter dependence upon the Lord Jesus.[2]

The mystery of faith was being unveiled to my sin-blinded eyes. What revolutionized my thinking was the Holy Spirit's anointing, enabling me to see how I could never save myself. The lie in the Garden, that I could make myself God-like through my own efforts, was exposed as a fraud by the Holy Spirit. What I did, or will do, cannot save. Only Jesus can save.

The light of the gospel poured into my soul and suddenly the Bible's message of salvation made perfect sense. God made the Path to salvation one that would not feed our boastful, self-loving pride. It is the only religious Path to salvation, the only therapeutic-spiritual course of treatment, that does not feed our disease.

"SO THAT NO ONE MAY BOAST"

Paul tells us that the *"unmerited favor"* of God—the definition of grace—is what saves us, and we receive this gift of "saving grace" through the gift of faith. We tend to focus on the all-important topics of grace and faith in the following verse about salvation, but the phrase that ends this verse shows us how the Path to Christlikeness does not allow us to take credit for any part of our salvation:

---

[1] Luther, *Commentary on Galatians*, p. 60
[2] Watchman Nee, *Sit, Walk, Stand* (Wheaton: Tyndale House Publishers, Inc., 1977), p. 15. Emphasis added.

> For by grace you have been saved through faith. And this is not your own doing; it is the gift of God, not a result of works, *so that no one may boast* (Eph 2:8-9; emphasis added).

Every other spiritual path requires a measure of self-salvation. They lead you to salvation, or enlightenment, through prayer, meditation, or some action—in Paul's terminology, through "works." Since you have a hand in your own salvation on these false paths, you've earned the right to be proud of your great achievement. But on the Way that is Christ, salvation is a gift of God. It is not the result of our will; it is the result of God's will:

> But to all who did receive him, who believed in his name, he *gave the right to become children of God*, who were born, not of blood nor of the will of the flesh *nor of the will of man, but of God* (Jn 1:12-13, emphasis added).

The desire to exalt oneself through one's own efforts was inspired by Satan, and resulted in the Fall. On the Path to Christlikeness, we play no role in our salvation.

WHERE SELF-SALVATION LEADS

Martin Luther understood, in the depths of his soul, how our own efforts cannot save us. As a conscience-stricken monk, he spent all of his energies trying to save himself by fulfilling the law through his own strength. He describes where this path leads:

> I tried hard to live up to every law as best I could. I punished myself with fasting, watching, praying and other exercises more than all those who today hate me and persecute me. I was so much in earnest that I imposed upon my body more than it could stand.
> ...Yet under the cloak of my outward respectability I continually mistrusted, doubted, feared, hated and blasphemed God. My righteousness was a filthy puddle. Satan loves such saints. They are his darlings, for they quickly destroy their body and soul by depriving them of the blessings of God's generous gifts.[3]

Instead of rest and peace, Luther's vain striving produced restlessness, doubt and fear. He tried to achieve salvation by living according to the Law, as he understood it, and he found that human effort could not achieve this end.

Adam is the exemplar of the futility of works. God told him, "...cursed is the ground because of you; in pain you shall eat of it all the

---

[3] Martin Luther, *Commentary on the Epistle to the Galatians*, pp 24. 25.

days of your life; thorns and thistles it shall bring forth for you..." (Gn 3:17-18). Instead of fruit, Adam's toil would produce thorns and thistles, a weed with sharp spines. His sin condemned him to live a fruitless life of toil under the sun, and then die. The Book of Ecclesiastes is his biography, and the epitaph of every fallen person is one of its opening lines, "Vanity of vanities! All is vanity" (Ec 1:2).

ASK YOURSELF...

When I was a Christian in name only, a real Christian asked me a question that I found difficult to answer, "When were you saved?" I offered him a word-salad that was not an answer, and the question kept echoing in my empty heart and mind.

Because it is an important question to answer on this side of the grave, I will now ask you, "When were you saved?"

If you say, "I don't know the exact moment, but I believe in Jesus. I accepted Him as my Lord and Savior over ten years ago," I would reply, "Excellent! Praise God! For you know what the state of your soul rests on, namely, a saving faith in Jesus."

Friends, you might not have experienced anything that communicated to your emotions or intellect that the Holy Spirit indwelt you when you came to a saving faith. Feelings and thoughts of confirmation are not required. What is required is faith, and the confession of this faith.

So, if you feel drawn to Jesus, and are uncertain of your salvation, then now is the time to say, "Lord Jesus, I believe in You. You are the good news. You died for me because You love me and I believe this to be true, for this gospel is found in the Word of God. You paid my debt on the cross. I am a child of God, now and forever, because of You, not because of me, and for that I give You thanks and praise. Amen."

If you were not a member before this moment, and you prayed this prayer from the heart, then I welcome you to the Body of Christ, and the adventure that lies ahead. It is a journey that will frequently be confusing, because God will turn your life upside-down and inside-out. But we have signposts, along the Path, to help guide us, and we will continue to explore their meaning.

The Feast of Passover marks the beginning of the Path to Christlikeness, but in order for us to become Christlike we need to destroy our old nature. This painful process begins in the wilderness which is represented by the second signpost on the Path, the Feast of Unleavened Bread. It is our next destination, and it introduces a change in our diet. We will discover what's on the menu in the next chapter.

2

THE FEAST OF UNLEAVENED BREAD

'

THE WILDERNESS

Faith in the blood of our Passover Lamb, Jesus, granted us access to the Path, and after we find our footing on it, we are led into the wilderness to start the next phase of our discipleship.

The Feast of Unleavened Bread was a celebration that began the day after Passover. Its focus was on departing from Egypt and an unusual diet:

> You shall eat no leavened bread with it. Seven days you shall eat it with unleavened bread, *the bread of affliction*—for you came out of the land of Egypt in haste—that all the days of your life you may remember the day when you came out of the land of Egypt (Dt 16:3, emphasis added).

The symbol of bread without leaven is rich in spiritual meaning. In the Bible "leaven" is often a symbol of sin. It works its way through the entire loaf and makes the bread expand through its influence. Its association with a boastful arrogance and pride—i.e., being "puffed up"—can be seen in the following verse: "Your boasting is not good. Do you not know that a little leaven leavens the whole lump?" (1 Cor 5:6).

Instead of being puffed up, unleavened bread is flat, because without the leavening agent it cannot rise. It is a symbol of humility and the experiences that deflate us. And eating "the bread of affliction" for seven days indicates it will be our diet until it accomplishes its purpose, for "seven" is the number of completion and fulfillment.

After Passover, the Israelites entered the wilderness, a spiritual training facility that was designed to humble them and test their faith:

> And you shall remember the whole way that the LORD your God
> has led you these forty years in the wilderness, that he might
> *humble you, testing you* to know what was in your heart... (Dt
> 8:2, emphasis added).

The wilderness was also designed to reduce them to complete dependence
on the grace of God. They became nomads living in temporary shelters
called tabernacles or booths. Being nomads, always on the move, they
could not raise crops like wheat to make bread. So, they were made to
depend on manna from heaven. Water was also in short supply in the
wilderness, so they became dependent on God's grace that gave them
water from a rock.

Year-after-year they were slowly being remade into the image of God.
The faithless generation who would not even attempt to take the Promised
Land, was being replaced by one endowed with the courage that comes
from trusting God and believing in His promises.

On the Path, we are like the Israelites in the wilderness. Our faith is
constantly being tested. Our old strength is withering away and being
replaced by a spiritual strength. Slowly but surely, the divine scalpel cuts
away everything in us that is not Christ. It is a painful operation, but one
that is necessary if we are to become Christlike.

THE THEOLOGY OF THE CROSS

The wilderness is a depiction of the surgical suite that is called the cross in
the New Testament. The cross is a symbol of self-denying humility. As
Jesus said, "If anyone would come after me, *let him deny himself* and take
up his cross *daily* and follow me" (Lk 9:23; emphasis added). One of the
primary ways this self-denial takes place is through a steady diet of the
bread of affliction, or suffering, and that brings us to Martin Luther's
theology of the cross.

Luther's "...theology of the cross views man as one who has been
called to suffer. Man's cross 'destroys man's self-confidence' so that now,
instead of wanting to do something himself, he allows God to do
everything in him."[1] Self-denial, suffering...welcome to the wilderness
and to the cross.

It is a tough process to endure. Luther may have described this stage
best when he wrote, "In this trial and struggle...the righteous man always
resembles more a loser than a victor, for the Lord lets him be tested and
assailed to his utmost limits as gold is tested in a furnace."[2]

---

[1] Paul Althus, *The Theology of Martin Luther*, trans. Robert C. Schultz
(Philadelphia: Fortress Press, 1966), p. 27-28.
[2] Quoted in Bloesch, v. 2, p. 35.

We are humbled so that we might be exalted by the hand of God, and we are emptied so that we might be filled by His Spirit. However, there is no getting around this fact: Being subjected to the cross is not easy or fun.

Jesus did not misrepresent this part of His training program. The following statement by Jesus is repeated in Scripture, in various forms, more often than any other, "For whoever would save his life will lose it, but whoever *loses his life* for my sake will find it" (Mt 16:25, emphasis added. See also Mt 10:39, Mk 8:35, Lk 9:24 and 17:33, and Jn 12:25).

We are back in the world of divine inversions. To save your life you must lose your life. The "old you" must die so that the "new you" can live and thrive. Again, with the exception of Caleb and Joshua, every adult Israelite who entered the wilderness died there, and the death of our old nature is what Jesus and our spiritual wilderness promises.

Think of "dying" in these terms: Our power declines so that we can express the power of God. Luther's theology of the cross puts it this way:

> He, however, who has emptied himself through suffering no longer does works, but knows that God works and does all things in him. For this reason, whether God does works or not, it is all the same to him. He neither boasts if he does good works, nor is he disturbed if God does not do good works through him. He knows that it is sufficient if he suffers and is brought low by the cross in order to be annihilated all the more.[3]

Luther is restating the truth Jesus repeated so often: "Whoever loses his life for my sake will find it." But the above quote almost sounds like Christians are perfectly serene while being operated on by the cross. Some may be, but when most of us are in this pitiless desert there are times when we can barely lift up our head.

We don't glory in the cross when we are being operated upon. God will take us to the point of capitulation and, depending on our condition, not just once, but several times during this sanctification process called "being discipled by Jesus."

The cross is remorseless in the way it brings us to unconditional surrender. We cling to a slender thread and place our hope in it, and then the thread breaks. We believe a new turn of events will finally improve our condition, and it leads to things worsening. Then, as the darkness exceeds anything we've ever experienced before, it gets darker still. None of our schemes work. Every attempt to leave this desert fails. We are abandoned in our sunless cage until we turn, unconditionally, to the Light of the world: Jesus. He is our portion and all we will ever need.

---

[3] Althus, p. 28.

As we stumble through the wilderness may these words fortify us with strength and hope.

> God does not give us, His children, what we deserve. (Because of our sin, we deserve His wrath.) When we are babes, He rarely gives us what we want. (What we desire, until we grow spiritually, is often detrimental.) But throughout the entirety of our lives, He gives us what we need, for our good. For the Path is designed to make us Christlike.

THE PROMISE OF SUFFERING

The promises of Jesus cover many areas of life, and among them is suffering. "In the world you will have tribulation" (Jn 16:33). Jesus does not say we might have tribulation, He promises we will have it. And we must patiently endure it, or we will be like the whining Israelites in the wilderness whose constant complaints angered God.

One thing is certain, we will reach a point where we feel we are spending too much time in the wilderness. But suffering is a required course in our discipleship-training program. If we are to be glorified with Christ, then we must also share in His sufferings:

> The Spirit himself bears witness with our spirit that we are children of God, and if children, then heirs—heirs of God and fellow heirs with Christ, *provided we suffer with him* in order that we may also be glorified with him (Ro 8:16-17, emphasis added).

We tend to skip over this bit about the necessity of suffering with Jesus, but the Path does not skip over it, nor will the lives of anyone walking upon the Path. Jesus suffered the cross for us, and every day He hands each of His disciples a cross so that they can suffer with Him.

Times of tribulation test our faith and expose the weakness of it. These seasons of suffering are designed to drive us to our knees in humility, and annihilate our faith-in-self. Suddenly, nothing we do in our own power works. Then, after we throw up our arms in despair, we turn to Jesus and our dependency on Him is strengthened. He is the bread of life, our manna from heaven, who will one day replace the bread of affliction with His loving, merciful Self.

THE NECESSITY OF OUR SOUL SURGERY

Until our faith-in-self is destroyed, we tend to believe we are the authors of our good fortune. If God blessed us before we were emptied of self, we would take credit for whatever His blessing produced. This would merely increase the self-exalting pride that the Path to Christlikeness is designed to destroy.

God's blessings can become curses when the self-centered nature is alive and well. For example, the person who has not been emptied of self, and inherits great wealth, is concerned with how he can use it to satisfy himself and not others. The parable of the Prodigal Son is an illustration of this. After he received his inheritance, he squandered it in a life of dissipation.

To enable us to be blest by His power without being cursed, Christ consigns us to the sterile, surgical suite called the wilderness to excise spiritual malignancies from our soul. The Prodigal Son, for example, was feeding pigs and starving to death prior to coming to his senses and returning to his father to receive riches and honor. He was humbled that he might be exalted.

THE MASTER GARDENER

The Bible has another word to describe how we will go under the knife and it is "pruning." Pruning is a word understood by gardeners. It refers to cutting away things like dead branches, or anything that interferes with increased fruitfulness.

Jesus told His apostles that He chose them and appointed them to go and bear fruit that would last, and that every branch that bore fruit would be pruned so that it would be even more fruitful. Not even the apostles of Jesus were exempt from pruning, or soul surgery. And just as Jesus is a master surgeon, reshaping our soul, He is also a master gardener, cutting off the unnecessary parts of our nature that hinder our fruitfulness.

As we stumble through the wilderness, we come to the realization that our walk of faith and the way of the cross are one. For we are to walk by faith every day, and also take up our cross daily.

Luther noted how the exercising of faith accomplishes what the cross does. He wrote: "…faith is denial of ourselves, total rejection of self and reliance on God's grace."[4] If we are to become truly Christlike, then our faith-in-Christ must replace our faith-in-self.

AFFLICTION: FAITH IN A TIME OF PLAGUE

The way we've individually and collectively responded to the Covid-19 plague revealed a lot about the strength or weakness of our faith. There are few faith-tests more humbling than to live during a time of plague.

A Christian named Cyprian, also discovered what life was like during a time of plague. He lived during the great pandemic that rattled the Roman Empire for about a dozen years (c. 250-262 AD). He wrote about

---

[4] Walter von Loewenich, *Luther's Theology of the Cross* tr. Herbert J. A. Bouman (Minneapolis: Augsburg Publishing House, 1976), p. 129.

the plague's horrors, and for his literary efforts was rewarded by having the pandemic named after him.

At the height of the Plague of Cyprian there were 5,000 deaths a day and the symptoms were horrific. People literally wasted away from round-the-clock vomiting and diarrhea. Some lost their sight and hearing. Infections were often followed by the rotting away of one's flesh and the amputation of these infected limbs.

The pagans in the Roman Empire—the majority of the population at that time—had their faith tested during the Plague of Cyprian and it failed. Instead of tending to their loved ones, to comfort them and alleviate their suffering, they would abandon them and allow them to die alone. To be around them increased their chances of contracting the plague. Their overpowering fear of death turned them into cowards who were incapable of compassion. In them we can see the self-centering effects of the fall.

The Christians, on the other hand, tended to their sick in an attempt to nurse them back to health and *to suffer with* them, the literal meaning of the word "compassion." And, to the amazement of the pagan Romans, they tended to some of the sick pagans as well.

As Cyprian wrote in his essay *De Mortalitate* (On Mortality):

> What a grandeur of spirit it is to struggle with all the powers of an unshaken mind against so many onsets of devastation and death! what sublimity, to stand erect amid the desolation of the human race, and not to lie prostrate with those who have no hope in God; but rather to rejoice, and to embrace the benefit of the occasion; that in thus bravely showing forth our faith, and by suffering endured, going forward to Christ by the narrow way that Christ trod, we may receive the reward of His life and faith according to His own judgment.[5]

The actions of the Christian's revealed their faith and exposed the hollowness of their pagan neighbor's beliefs. They were a sham, providing them no support in their time of greatest need. As they witnessed the response of Christians to the plague, many pagans came to a saving faith. They could see how they did not have what the Christians had, and they wanted it. Christians, the salt of the earth, engendered a thirst for the Living Water of Christ.

The Path is designed to give us a faith that remains strong during a plague year, because it makes "faith" our life's work. As Jesus said, "This

---

[5] Cyprian, *De Mortalitate*. Transl. Ernest Wallis, (Grand Rapids, MI: Christian Classics Ethereal Library,).

is the work of God, that you believe in him whom he has sent" (Jn 6:29). Our work is believing in Jesus, resting in Jesus, and relying on His grace.

WEAKEN THE OLD SELF, STRENGTHEN THE NEW

Many Christians quote Friedrich Nietzsche's famous epigram, "What does not destroy me, makes me stronger," and agree with its message. But on the Christian Path, we are weakened by our trials, so that we might turn to Jesus and be endowed with His strength.

Nietzsche, author of *The Anti-Christ* and other Christ-despising works, was Satan's philosopher, and his works express his father's philosophy. Man, according to Nietzsche, is just a step toward life's ultimate goal: Becoming the Superman. He takes us back to the Garden of Eden with the promise that we will be like God, and then he added for good measure, "God is dead." This dead "God" needed to be replaced, and who was better suited to do so than a supremely arrogant "Superman."

Nietzsche's epigram sounds heroic to many Christians. It paints this picture: I struggle, perhaps get knocked down many times, and rise up mightier than before. However, Scripture rejects the world's vision of heroism. It chooses the least promising people to be its heroes so that no one will give them the glory that belongs to God.

In the Bible's pantheon of heroes, we find people like Gideon. He was so low on Israel's totem pole that he could not believe the Angel of the Lord when he was told he would deliver Israel from the hand of the Midianites. When told this he replied:

> "Please, Lord, how can I save Israel? Behold, my clan is the weakest in Manasseh, and I am the least in my father's house." And the LORD said to him, "But I will be with you, and you shall strike the Midianites as one man" (Jdg 6:15-16).

There is a reason for the popularity of cartoon figures like the Incredible Hulk, or Superman, and mythological figures like Hercules and Thor. With their bulging muscles and ferocity, they are the world's vision of power. But when the Bible portrays its lone strong man, Samson, it has him being defeated by a woman.

The Bible's heroes are typically like David, a puny shepherd with a bag of rocks. What made David much stronger than Goliath was his unshakable faith in God's power. He knew his God was stronger than any giant. He believed God could and would deliver this giant into his hands.

THE STRONG ARE MADE WEAK

Being a weak person is not a prerequisite for being selected by God to advance His Kingdom. Some of God's servants were strong-willed people, highly educated and richly gifted when they started their work for Him. The Apostle Paul was such a person. Before his conversion, he exuded strength and self-confidence. Then, after his conversion, he recalled just how full of himself he was:

> If anyone else thinks he has reason for confidence in the flesh, I have more: circumcised on the eighth day, of the people of Israel, of the tribe of Benjamin, a Hebrew of Hebrews; as to the law, a Pharisee; as to zeal, a persecutor of the church; as to righteousness under the law, blameless (Ph 3:4-6).

Paul's confidence in his standing with God, apart from Christ, needed to be destroyed. Like every other fallen person, Paul needed to change the orientation of his soul to Christ-confidence and Christ-reliance. For one so full of himself, this would require substantial servings of the bread of affliction. So, immediately after Paul's conversion, Jesus said, "I will show him how much he must suffer for the sake of my name" (Ac 9:16).

Paul was not being punished for his crimes against the church. His sins were forgiven. Instead, Paul was sent down the way of the cross so that he might receive unimaginable blessings. After Paul received a thorn in his flesh to keep him from becoming conceited, he asked Jesus to remove it three times. Jesus refused to remove it because He wanted Paul to continue in His power. He told Paul, "My grace is sufficient for you, for my power is made perfect in weakness" (2 Cor 12:9). And Paul's response to this reveals the nature of grace in this world of divine inversion:

> Therefore I will boast all the more gladly of my weaknesses, so that the power of Christ may rest upon me. For the sake of Christ, then, I am content with weaknesses, insults, hardships, persecutions, and calamities. *For when I am weak, then I am strong* (2 Cor 12: 9-10, emphasis added).

When you are going through difficulties—and you will on the Path— remember the above verse. In your weakened state, reliant on Christ's grace, you are now stronger than you would be on your own. Our world is being turned upside-down by God so that it might finally be right-side-up.

JACOB THE DECEIVER

Jacob lived by his wits, always scheming to get ahead. He took advantage of Esau's hunger to steal his birthright. Later, Jacob deceived his father, Isaac, into believing he was Esau, so that he would receive the blessing reserved for the first-born. Following this he struggled with his father-in-law Laban, a talented schemer, who met his match in Jacob.

Once Jacob escaped his virtual enslavement to Laban, he faced a dangerous situation. He would have to travel through the lands where Esau dwelt. Esau wanted to kill Jacob for deceiving him (see Gen 27:36), and Jacob was filled with dread at the thought of meeting his brother. So, he concocted the following scheme to secure his brother's favor. He would send servants ahead of him and they were to give Esau much of his livestock and the message, "They belong to your servant Jacob. They are a present sent to my lord Esau. And moreover, he is behind us" (Gen 32:18).

If Jacob turned to God in prayer for the grace to overcome the challenge of meeting Esau, then Scripture fails to record this. More than likely, he did not turn to God for help. "Self" was Jacob's north star, and if it required deception to get what he wanted, then he was okay with that. God now entered Jacob's life to save him from himself.

The night before his meeting with Esau, Jacob sent his family and possessions ahead so that he was alone. Then the story takes a strange turn. All of the sudden he is wrestling with a man until daybreak and it turns out this man is God. God, the maker of heaven and earth, obviously could win any wrestling match. But that was not His purpose, weakening Jacob was. So, God touched Jacob's hip socket so that his hip was wrenched and afterwards he limped.

Of the three patriarchs, Jacob is the one most like us. His faith in God appears to be small when compared to his faith-in-self. It is a habitual orientation of the fallen nature that must be broken in all of us.

WHAT'S IN A NAME?

Jacob knew he needed the blessing of God, so he refused to let the man go until he received it. But God is the one who dictates terms. He asked Jacob, "What is your name" (Gen 32:27)? This is akin to demanding of Jacob that he admit defeat, or say, "Uncle!" Jacob surrendered his name.

God then made sure Jacob understood he was now reporting to Him, and communicated this by giving him a new name: "Israel." When a person names someone, as a parent names a child, it indicates his authority over him or her. God changed Jacob's name to *Israel*, meaning, "he struggles with God," and declared that he had struggled with God, and man, and had prevailed.

This is how we prevail with God: We cling to Him while we are wrestling with Him and He weakens us. Our battle-cry needs to be, "Though he slay me, I will hope in him" (Job 13:15). We do not let Him go, and we submit to His authority. Humble submission is one way we worship the Father and Christ, and it is the subject of the next chapter.

3

THE FEAST OF FIRSTFRUITS

FIRSTFRUITS

At every stage on the Path, we offer the fruit of our labors to the glory of God, because once we are on the Way, the days of Adam, of fruitless toil under the sun, are over. During the Feast of Firstfruits a worshipper would give the priest the firstfruits, or initial produce, of the barley harvest.

This offering of firstfruits acknowledges a spiritual truth: All that we are, all that we produce, everything belongs to the Lord, and God is to have priority in all things. This priority extends to the earliest stages of the harvest, and to the firstborn of animals and humans. As God commanded, "Whatever is the first to open the womb among the people of Israel, both of man and of beast, is mine" (Ex 13:2).

However, after the Fall, the firstfruits of Eve's womb was Cain, the murderer of his brother Abel. Cain should have belonged to God, but instead, he belonged to Satan. As the Apostle John noted: "We should not be like Cain, who was of the evil one and murdered his brother" (1 Jn 3:12). Spiritually speaking, Satan was Cain's father. The created order was upside down and this required a divine inversion. But first, let's answer the question, "What caused Cain's murderous rage?"

Cain and Abel played two different roles. We read, "Abel was a keeper of sheep, and Cain a worker of the ground" (Gen 4:2). When it came time to make an offering, God looked favorably on Abel's offering of the first-born of his flock, but did not look favorably on Cain's offering of grain. This enraged Cain.

According to Hebrews, "By faith Abel offered to God a more acceptable sacrifice than Cain, through which he was commended as righteous" (Heb 11:4). Abel was faithful and deemed righteous, and this made his offering acceptable, but Cain had a sin problem. God told Cain, "If you do well, will you not be accepted? And if you do not do well, sin is crouching at the door. Its desire is contrary to you, but you must rule over it" (Gen 4:7).

The acceptance of Cain's sacrifice was based on whether he was righteous or sinful, faithful or unfaithful, whether he did well or not, rather than being based on what he was offering. Furthermore, God warned Cain that sin was about to take control of him and added, "the desire of sin is against you," because sin is never for you. It injures the soul. God's righteous commands are for our good.

After Abel was murdered, and Cain was exiled, Adam and Eve were without a son, and they did not call on the name of the Lord. This meant Adam and Eve were failing to offer another type of fruit to God.

THE FRUIT OF OUR LIPS

The author of Hebrews wrote, "Through him [i.e., Jesus—my note] then let us continually offer up a sacrifice of praise to God, that is, the fruit of lips that *acknowledge his name*" (Heb 13:15, emphasis added).

If our words of praise are like fruit, then after our salvation, what are the firstfruits of our lips that we offer to God? The Apostle Paul ties the words we speak to our salvation-justification, "For with the heart one believes and is justified, and with the mouth one confesses and is saved" (Ro 10:10).

After the Holy Spirit enters our heart, one of the firstfruits of our saved soul is the confession, "Jesus is Lord," because we have accepted Him as our Lord and Savior. It is like our signature on a new covenant, finalizing the agreement, and sealing our relationship with God. These words come from the Spirit that now indwells us:

> Therefore I want you to understand that no one speaking in the Spirit of God ever says "Jesus is accursed!" and no one can say "Jesus is Lord" except in the Holy Spirit (1 Co 12:3).

After the Fall, Adam and Eve failed to "acknowledge His name." Perhaps it was their sorrow that turned them inward. But after the birth of their son, Seth, and Seth's son, Enosh, "people began to call upon the name of the LORD" (Gn 4:26). The Holy Spirit moved them to acknowledge their God as LORD, and with this the lineage of Adam returned to worshipping their Maker, and offering Him the firstfruits of their lips and heart.

WORSHIPPING GOD

The word "worship" means bowing down in reverence to someone. It is an attitude of submission, a physical expression declaring, "I am Your servant." And it is not an option; worshipping God is a requirement on the Path. The Israelites were freed from slavery to end their service to Pharaoh and begin their life of service and submission to God (Ex 10:3). And we who walk the Path are like the Israelites who were freed from slavery, for we also are required to bow down before God and humbly submit to serving Him. As Paul wrote:

> I appeal to you therefore, brothers, by the mercies of God, to present your bodies as *a living sacrifice*, holy and acceptable to God, which is *your spiritual worship*. (Ro 12:1, emphasis added).

Worship, service, becoming living sacrifices… no matter where we are on the Path, the cross is not far from us, and we become the firstfruits offered to God. This offering of ourselves to God acknowledges and confirms the fact that we belong to Him.

JEREMIAH LANPHIER AND A WORSHIPFUL LIFE

To the fallen heart, a servant's life sounds awful. But we are living in a world of inversion, where to turn everything upside-down is to turn it right-side-up. On the Path we discover the key to living a meaningful and happy life is through serving God, which is to worship Him.

Such a blessed life is illustrated by Jeremiah Lanphier. He was a lay-missionary, living in New York City, and was hired to turn around the declining attendance of the Fulton Street Church. His job was to go from house to house and encourage the un-churched to attend Fulton Street.

As his work was met with a discouraging lack of success, he turned to God in prayer and continually asked, "Lord, what wilt Thou have me to do?" If it was the Lord's will, he was okay with continuing this apparently fruitless enterprise, and this attitude sums up the life of a worshipper. It is a surrendered life that gives priority to God's agenda and His timing.

I've worked many years in the world of business. In it you can find seminars teaching attendees how to ask good questions to uncover invaluable information affecting marketing, sales, employee morale and much else. In the world of sanctification asking good questions is even more important, because it can impact our spiritual fruitfulness and that has eternal implications. Lanphier's question, in modern English—Lord, what would You have me do—is an excellent question to ask God.

Then, when you feel you've received an answer, a good follow-up question is, "Is this [insert task] what You would have me do?" As we become sensitive to the promptings of the Spirit, we will either feel at peace with a task, or uneasy about focusing our time and attention on it.

One day Lanphier's question received a cryptic answer, "God wants the people to pray." He did not hear a voice. It was not a thought that firmly gripped his mind, refusing to let it wander anywhere else. Nothing about this thought bore the signs of an answer from God. Instead, it was a passing thought that came to him during the course of his workday. Then it slowly grew stronger until he could no longer avoid responding to it. No follow-up question was needed in this case. God was saying, "Do it! And do it now."

DISCERNING GOD'S WILL

A plan of action began to form in Lanphier's mind. He would start holding flexible prayer meetings during the lunch hour to meet the needs of businessmen in the neighborhood. It would include singing, exhortation, and prayer.

His friends were not enthusiastic about the program and only six people attended the first session. Undeterred by this modest start, Lanphier continued to hold meetings because he believed this is what God wanted him to do, and the meetings that followed kept growing.

Soon weekly meetings became daily meetings, and then the daily meetings could not hold the large crowds so these prayer warriors spilled into other churches to pray. The prayer meetings then spread to Philadelphia, Boston, Chicago, and to small towns and cities across the U.S. They spread to Northern Ireland, Wales, England, Scotland, continental Europe, South Africa, India and Australia, and as a result, hundreds of thousands came to a saving faith in Jesus Christ. It was a revival of a breadth and intensity that is rarely seen.

Obviously, Lanphier was not responsible for the glorious outpouring of God's Spirit in New York City and elsewhere. But God's will ordained that this spiritual conflagration would not start until someone struck a match, and that privilege was extended to Jeremiah Lanphier, a man few people have heard of.

This revival was like the Reformation, though on a much smaller scale. According to the will of God, the Reformation was going to happen. Nothing could stop it. But the privilege of initiating this massive outpouring of God's Spirit was given to Martin Luther.

A surrendered life is challenging. I am sure Lanphier wondered from time to time, "What am I doing Lord? I seem to be marching in place, going nowhere." But he remained surrendered and desirous of learning what it was that God would have him do. When God finally sent him in a seemingly inconsequential direction he trusted and obeyed, and this is the essence of the Path to Christlikeness.

Lanphier seemed to be marking time prior to the prayer revival, and perhaps he was. Sometimes the cross operates on us by forcing us to wait, and everyone must attend the school of discipline known as "waiting." Its lessons are invaluable and the Puritan poet, John Milton, understood this. The final line of his magnificent poem, *On His Blindness*, reads, "They also serve who only stand and wait." I vividly remember how this line made absolutely no sense to me during those years when I was trying to save myself. Thankfully, now it does.

THE TASK GIVEN TO ANANIAS

For God's plan of salvation to be fulfilled, *according to His will*, He seeks worshippers who will bow down before Him and dedicate themselves to fulfilling His desires and not their own. They must trust Him even when their reason shouts, "God, You must be mistaken!" The story of Ananias and the Apostle Paul illustrates this.

Ananias was a disciple of Jesus who lived in Damascus. In a vision, the Lord said his name and he responded, "Here I am, Lord" (Ac 9:10). Then Jesus gave him an assignment to do the unimaginable: "Go find Saul, the murderous persecutor of the church, in the house of a man named Judas, who lives on Straight Street. Then lay your hands on him and heal him."

Ananias's response was, "Lord, I have heard from many about this man, how much evil he has done to your saints at Jerusalem. And here he has authority from the chief priests to bind all who call on your name" (Ac 9:13-14).

He was not telling Jesus, "No. I won't do it." He was simply saying, "This command of Yours makes no sense." When our finite mind meets God's infinite mind, much seems incoherent to us. So, the Lord explained why Saul, who would become the Apostle Paul, needed to be healed. Jesus was choosing him to serve as His apostle to the nations, or Gentiles. God's plan of salvation was entering a new phase. The direction of human history was about to change.

Submission to the will of God can take us down paths that make no sense, but what is required is faith, trust in the One who is giving us His orders. When we follow this simple Path, our lives will abound in fruitfulness. It is hard to imagine being fruitful in this arid wilderness, but upon salvation, through the grace of Christ, we were given spiritual gifts, divinely anointed capabilities that we must put to work.

INVESTING OUR TALENTS

Jesus told a parable about the Kingdom of Heaven and it began with a man distributing large sums of money to his three servants before going on a journey. He gave one servant five talents, another received two, and the third servant received one. After distributing this money, the master left his servants and expected them to put it to work.

He then returned to receive an accounting of their investments. Two of his servants doubled their money and were told, "Well done, good and faithful servant. You have been *faithful over a little*; I will set you over much. Enter into the joy of your master" (Mt 25:21, emphasis added). But the servant who received one talent did not put it to work. He hid it and gave it back to his master. For being unfaithful "over a little," he had his talent taken away and was cast into the darkness.

As a result of this parable, the word "talent" came to mean a natural aptitude, or gift, because the "talents" of money in this parable symbolize our spiritual gifts. We are given divinely anointed capabilities to serve God in small ways, and if we do so, we will be given much larger responsibilities in the Kingdom of God (in Luke's version of this parable the faithful stewards were put in charge of cities). We also get to enter the joy of our master, in part, because using our gifts is inherently enjoyable.

A. W. TOZER'S GIFTS AND CALLINGS

Sometimes the profitable use of our talent requires us to be careful stewards of our time. We cannot engage in every opportunity to serve that presents itself. To do so might result in engaging in fruitless tasks. The pastoral service of A. W. Tozer illustrates this principle.

Tozer was called by God to communicate His truth through the pulpit and by writing simply and beautifully. These tasks require a great amount of time and energy. So, to be fruitful in both tasks, he had to protect how he spent his time.

When a church on the south side of Chicago sought to hire him as their pastor, he made the following stipulation: I accept so long as I am not a visitation pastor. This meant that one set of duties—visiting shut-in members, those who are grieving or are in need of support, the sick who are in hospitals, etc.—would fall to others. They agreed to his condition.

Was Tozer being selfish? Don't people within the church need this ministry of mercy and compassion? Yes, and the church is better served when someone who is spiritually gifted in those areas is performing these tasks. The visitation duties would have taken time away from areas of Tozer's giftedness, and likely would have drained him of the energy he needed to fulfill his calling. To spend large amounts of time in an area we aren't passionate about, or gifted in, is exhausting. Tozer was simply obeying the message of Christ's parable: Invest your talent wisely.

THE BIBLE'S LISTS OF GIFTS

The Bible contains several gift lists (see Rom 12, 1 Cor 12, Eph 4:7-12, 1 Pt 4:10-11), and the gifts within them are: Administration, being an apostle, discernment, evangelism, exhortation, faith, giving, healing, helps, hospitality, knowledge, leadership, mercy, prophecy, serving, speaking in tongues, teaching and wisdom.

These lists do not contain every spiritual gift. For example, in these lists we find the gift of faith, but where is the gift of hope? We find the gift of wisdom, but where is the gift of understanding? Where is courage, perseverance or patience?

The lack of comprehensiveness does not mean these New Testament gift lists are without value, but it does suggest a flaw in the methodology of some tools that are designed to help you discover your gifts, but are limited to these lists.

DISCOVER YOUR GIFTS

To discover your spiritual gifts, I recommend using secular assessments that determine what your talents are. Their "talent" lists are more comprehensive than the gift lists in the Bible. Also, the methodology and questions these secular assessments use to determine your talents have been tested. This scientific vetting is a time-consuming, expensive process, but it ensures a degree of accuracy that many Christian assessment tools, with their limited funding, might not have.

The question becomes, "Are these talents the same things as 'spiritual' gifts?"

Talents are wonderful endowments, and I believe all good things come from God. The case of Saul of Tarsus—aka the Apostle Paul— illustrates how the talents we possess prior to salvation can be anointed by God to become spiritual gifts.

Before being saved by grace, Saul/Paul possessed the gift of leadership. He was a leader of the movement to suppress Christianity, and higher-ranking Jewish leaders expressed their confidence in Saul's leadership abilities by giving him great authority.

Was this tremendous leadership ability of Saul's, then anointed and made even more fruitful after his conversion? Undoubtedly. He led the development of the church outside of Israel, and developed its leadership structure of elders and deacons, as well as their qualifications. When God anoints us with power it is not to obliterate our personality, but to reform it and work through it.

Paul also had the gift of "knowledge" before his conversion. He was a zealous student of the Torah and was gifted in this area of scriptural knowledge. But after the Spirit anointed his mind, he had a divinely-inspired knowledge that can only come from God. His understanding of the Bible, and what it said about the Christ, underwent a revolution that led him into a deeper understanding of God's Word than probably anyone before him, other than Jesus, His Teacher.

God wants our best. That means He wants us to engage our talents, or what we do best, so that we can be productive members of the Kingdom. So, discover what your gifts are and start using them. One of the better assessments of our talents is free. Go to "viacharacter.org" and take their free survey to start this process of self-discovery.

Discovering your strengths can also help your career. For no matter what we do, we cannot *intentionally* utilize our talents unless we know what they are. And here is the beauty of engaging them. According to the Gallup organization, our strengths/talents are those things that we do consistently at a near-perfect level, and that we can see ourselves doing repeatedly and enjoyably. Our strengths became so, in part, because we enjoyed using them. Our serving the Kingdom through the gifts God gave us is meant to be a joyful exercise, and intentionally engaging our talents can make our careers more fruitful and enjoyable as well.

FIRSTFRUITS AND PENTECOST

Passover is a symbol of Jesus' crucifixion and Firstfruits is a symbol of His resurrection. Firstfruits occurred on the third day of the Passover Festival, and it was the day Jesus resurrected from the grave. Paul alluded to this when he wrote, "But in fact Christ has been raised from the dead, the firstfruits of those who have fallen asleep" (1 Cor 15:20).

The Feast of Firstfruits is a reminder that our time spent in the wilderness enables us to express the power of Christ's resurrection by producing a rich harvest. Note the connection made between suffering (pruning?) and fruitfulness:

> For they [our earthly fathers] disciplined us for a short time as it seemed best to them, but he [our heavenly Father] disciplines us for our good, *that we may share his holiness*. For the moment all discipline seems painful rather than pleasant, but later it *yields the peaceful fruit of righteousness* to those who have been trained by it (Heb 12:10-11, emphasis and bracketed notes added).

The wilderness, or the cross, is for our good so "that we may share his holiness." In other words, it is to make us Christlike. The author of Hebrews goes on to write, "For the moment all discipline seems painful." To that I say, "There is no training program on earth that can match the toughness of the one developed by Jesus."

I was an Infantry Officer in the U.S. Army and graduated from both Airborne and Ranger School. To pass these programs we had to adopt the following attitude that uses the inelegant language of a soldier: "You can make me puke and pass out, but you can't make me quit."

These programs were tough, but when compared to the school Christ puts His soldiers through, they were relatively easy. Our spiritual training also requires an "I will never quit" attitude, and yet, fortified by the grimmest determination, we can still be made to say, "Uncle!" For we are not wrestling with some Drill Instructor, but with God, and the outcome of every match is the weakening of self.

The severity of the training program depends upon the condition of the sinner whom God is transforming into Christ's likeness. Returning to the Apostle Paul, prior to salvation he was, spiritually speaking, an absolute mess. He was an enemy of Christ and a persecutor of Christ's brothers and sisters. It took many rounds of reconstructive surgery to make him Christlike, and he recounts some of his suffering in these words:

> Are they servants of Christ? I am a better one—I am talking like a madman—with far greater labors, far more imprisonments, with countless beatings, and often near death. Five times I received at the hands of the Jews the forty lashes less one. Three times I was beaten with rods. Once I was stoned. Three times I was shipwrecked; a night and a day I was adrift at sea; on frequent journeys, in danger from rivers, danger from robbers, danger from my own people, danger from Gentiles, danger in the city, danger in the wilderness, danger at sea, danger from false brothers; in toil and hardship, through many a sleepless night, in hunger and thirst, often without food, in cold and exposure (2 Cor 11:23-27).

These terrible afflictions came from the hand of God. They might seem excessive and cruel. But we must always remember, the Lord loved Paul and gave him great honors. However, He knew how the former persecutor of Christians needed to be turned inside-out. On a person who was as fallen as Paul, this would require many painful operations. So, when we are feeling the lash of God's discipline, then we must understand that it is being lovingly administered "for our good, that we may share his holiness."

God is developing soldiers of the cross who can endure tremendous hardships and still wield their weapons of love and the Word of God, both in season and out of season. He is also preparing us for the second stage wherein we are clothed with spiritual power to serve God mightily and produce a rich harvest of spiritual fruit.

STAGE TWO:

HOPE

4

THE FEAST OF PENTECOST

EXPECTING TO BE SPIRIT-FILLED

FAITH AND HOPE

When faith becomes expectant it becomes hopeful, for hope is expectant faith. Hope looks forward to the future and *believes* that God's promises will be honored. A Christian is promised heaven, for example, and his hope of heaven sustains him as he makes his arduous pilgrimage to the Celestial City.

Martin Luther noted the similarity between faith and hope, and their differences as well:

> The question occurs to us, What difference is there between faith and hope. We find it difficult to see any difference. Faith and hope are so closely linked that they cannot be separated. Still there is a difference between them.
>
> …Faith is a judge. It judges errors. Hope is a soldier. It fights against tribulations, the Cross, despondency, despair, and waits for better things to come in the midst of evil. Without hope faith cannot endure. …By faith we begin, by hope we continue.[1]

In faith we are recruited into God's army, and in hope we march forth, expecting to accomplish great things through the power of God. Hope's motto was coined by the Father of Modern Missions, William Carey, who said: Expect great things from God; attempt great things for God.

---

[1] Martin Luther, *Commentary on the Epistle to the Galatians*

Like faith, hope is acquainted with the invisible world. Faith does not live by sight, and neither does hope:

> Now hope that is seen is not hope. For who hopes for what he sees? But if we hope for what we do not see, *we wait for it with patience* (Ro 8:24-25, emphasis added).

The words, "we wait for it," reveal the futuristic orientation of hope. And waiting patiently for something is believing the object of one's hope will come to pass. We see this expectant, trusting faith in the apostles who received a parting promise from Jesus.

PENTECOST: BEING FILLED WITH THE SPIRIT

Just before Jesus ascended into heaven, He promised His disciples:

> But *you will receive power* when the Holy Spirit has come upon you, and you will be my witnesses in Jerusalem and in all Judea and Samaria, and to the end of the earth (Ac 1:8, emphasis added).

When someone who is trustworthy promises us something, we have the expectation that it will be fulfilled, and there is no one more trustworthy than Jesus. He is the basis of the realization of all promises in a believer's life: "For all the promises of God find their Yes in him" (2 Cor 1:20).

Biblical hope is faith in the promises of God. The Lord promised the disciples they would be baptized by the Holy Spirit and they confidently waited for this to occur. Jesus' promise was realized ten days later when the Feast of Pentecost arrived. The Bible describes this Spirit-baptism as being "filled with the Holy Spirit" (Ac 2:4). It appeared as tongues of fire descending upon the disciples, and with it came the supernatural ability to communicate the gospel in foreign tongues.

This little band of Christ-worshippers numbered 120 souls, but immediately after being baptized by the Holy Spirit, Peter's sermon added 3000 people to their ranks. Some theologians call this moment the birthday of the church. I prefer to think of it as the day when, in the name of Jesus, the evangelistic conquest of the planet began.

Peter's sermon was not particularly eloquent. Nor was it persuasive in a worldly sense. It did not make an appeal to the egos of those listening. If anything, it was accusatory. His last sentence was, "Let all the house of Israel therefore know for certain that God has made him both Lord and Christ, this Jesus whom you crucified" (Ac 2:36). But it did appeal to the Word of God, and the way Scripture attested to Jesus being the Christ.

But even this appeal to God's Word, if it was not undergirded by the power of the Holy Spirit, would have failed. Did not Satan appeal to Scripture when he tempted Jesus? The Spirit must anoint the Word of God to make it overpowering, and we see this in Peter's sermon. The Holy Spirit filled Peter to the point of overflowing the banks of his soul, and his sermon became irresistibly powerful.

THE TWO WORKINGS OF THE SPIRIT

This Spirit-filling at Pentecost is not the same thing as being indwelt by the Holy Spirit at the time of our salvation. The indwelling of the Holy Spirit takes place one time, by grace through the gift of faith, while the Spirit-filling can occur many times.

Once God takes up residence in our bodies, turning us into a temple of the Holy Spirit, He does not leave. He now owns us. As Scripture declares, "Or do you not know that your body is a temple of the Holy Spirit within you, whom you have from God? You are not your own, for you were bought with a price" (1 Cor 6:19-20). This is the indwelling.

But the Bible records how Peter was filled with the Holy Spirit at Pentecost (Ac 2:4). Later on, he was filled again (Ac 4:8), and a short while after that he was filled by the Spirit once again (Ac 4:31).

Passover represents our being indwelt by the Holy Spirit, and adopted into the family of God. But Pentecost represents our being Spirit-filled in order to serve God even more mightily than before, through the power of the Spirit.

PENTECOST AND PRAYER

What were the disciples doing during this time between the promise of Spirit baptism and its realization? We find them "devoting themselves to prayer" (Ac 1:14). There is a strong connection between being Spirit-filled and prayer. Not only did the disciples focus on prayer prior to being Spirit-filled, they committed themselves to prayer afterwards. They delegated the duties of food distribution to others so that they could dedicate themselves "to prayer and to the ministry of the word" (Ac 6:4).

We are commanded to be filled with the Spirit, and it is associated with worshipful activities like singing spiritual hymns and prayers of thanksgiving:

> And do not get *drunk with wine*, for that is debauchery, but *be filled with the Spirit*, addressing one another in psalms and hymns and spiritual songs, singing and making melody to the Lord with your heart, giving thanks always and for everything to God the Father in the name of our Lord Jesus Christ, submitting to one another out of reverence for Christ (Eph 5:18-21, emphasis added).

Even getting "drunk with wine," in the above quote, is associated with Pentecost, because after the disciples were filled with the Holy Spirit, they appeared to be inebriated to those who saw them (Ac 2:13). The disciples were filled with joy, and the merriment they expressed made them appear to be drunk to others, an accusation that Peter quickly refuted.

TWO BAPTISMS

Our salvation is associated with the sacrament of *water-baptism*, because it illustrates how our saving faith in Jesus cleanses us of sin's stain. Depending on your denomination, this baptism often follows one's coming to a saving faith. The Anabaptist denomination called it the "believer's baptism."

The second stage of our journey involves being *baptized by the Holy Spirit* for the purpose of ministering in God's power. It is a different operation of the Spirit and a different baptism. It anoints us with divine power so that we serve God in His might and not our own. We are not Spirit-filled to merely make us feel good, but to share this Life with others. We see this in the way we are filled to overflowing.

> Whoever believes in me, as the Scripture has said, "Out of his heart will flow rivers of living water" (Jn 7:38).

Let's look at how this Spirit baptism plays out in the life of D. L. Moody. It illustrates how being filled with the Spirit can empower a Christian to expect great things from God, and attempt great things for God. But first, he was prepared for this anointing by the wilderness.

D. L. MOODY'S BAPTISM BY THE HOLY SPIRIT

MOODY'S HUMBLE ORIGIN

D. L. Moody grew up in poverty and his formal education ended in fifth grade. As a young adult his writing style was marked by misspellings, grammatical errors, and the sort of mistakes found among those who are one step removed from functional illiteracy. In the world's judgment, Moody was not "the pick of the litter," which made him a perfect choice to serve God in His power.

In 1855, when he was eighteen years old, his Sunday school teacher, Edward Kimball, visited him at his place of work and shared with him the good news of Jesus' love. Moody accepted the Lord as his Savior, and he was indwelt by the Holy Spirit.

The following year, he relocated to the city of Chicago. Shortly after arriving, he set out to serve the children of drug addicts, alcoholics, and broken homes who congregated on the Sands, which was located just north of the Chicago River on Lake Michigan's shoreline.

In 1858 he rented a vacant saloon and conducted Sunday school classes in it. In 1864 he founded the Illinois Street Church so that his Sunday school students could have a church where they felt more at home.

Here we see a man who was dedicating his life to the service of the Lord. He was leading people to Christ. He was a believer who was indwelt by the Spirit of God. However, he had yet to experience his personal Pentecost.

A SERVANT WHO NEEDED TO BE BROKEN

Moody's life was producing firstfruits, and he was faithfully offering them to God, but he knew something was holding him back. His spiritual condition was visible to other saints as well. Though born again, Moody's old nature refused to die. Sarah Cooke may have summed it up best in her *Wayside Sketches*: "Mr. Moody was an earnest, whole-souled worker, but ever to me there seemed such a lack in his words. It seemed more the human, the natural energy and force of character of the man, than anything spiritual."[2]

Because she recognized this, she and her friend, Ms. W. R. Hawxhurst, began praying for Moody. Moody knew they were praying for him, because every time he finished preaching, they told him so.

This offended his pride to the point where he became annoyed with their concern. He told them to pray for the unsaved, but these women refused to back down. They replied, "We are praying that you may get the power."[3] By this one can assume they meant the power that attends being baptized by the Holy Spirit.

Now, with merciful intent, God sent Moody into the wilderness. The great Chicago fire of 1871 destroyed most of the city including all that Moody had built up for God. The Illinois Street Church, the second Farwell Hall for his YMCA work, and his home that he had received as a gift, were all gone. He was crushed by his losses.

This was followed by the hard work of rebuilding, and that required money. But Moody, a great money-raiser for evangelical causes, could not muster the motivation to do this. His recollection of this time expressed his despair:

---

[2] Quoted in Warren W. Wiersbe, *Living With the Giants* (Grand Rapids: Baker Book House, 1993), p. 97.
[3] Lyle W. Dorsett, *A Passion for Souls: The Life of D. L. Moody* (Chicago: Moody Press, 1997), p. 150.

My heart was not in the work of begging. I could not appeal. I was crying all the time that God fill me with His Spirit.

...God seemed to be just showing me myself. I found I was ambitious; I was not preaching for Christ; I was preaching for ambition. ...For four months wrestling went on in me. I was a miserable man.[4]

Moody was wrestling with God in the wilderness and, as always, God was winning, weakening his old nature. God was holding up a mirror to Moody's soul and forcing him to look at himself without filters or pretense. Note also how his prayers to be filled with the Spirit preceded the actual event. Abandoning his pride, he even approached Cooke and Hawxhurst and asked if he might pray with them. They happily invited him to join them in prayer.

MOODY'S PENTECOST

Moody was walking down New York City's Wall Street mulling over the impotence of his preaching and his inability to raise funds, when the Spirit of God was poured out on him:

"Oh, what a day!" he later reported. "I cannot describe it; I seldom refer to it; it is almost too sacred an experience to name... I can only say that God revealed Himself to me, and I had such an experience of His love that I had to ask Him to stay His hand."[5]

We enter the wilderness to prepare us for the baptism of the Holy Spirit. Moody experienced an infinitesimal, utterly overwhelming portion of God's glory. He enjoyed a level of communion that few attain.

Dr. Stanley Gundry wrote:

Moody seldom went into the details of his 1871 experience, or at least existing sermons seldom give the details, but on those rare occasions when he did, he described it as a filling, a baptism or an anointing that came upon him when he was in a cold state. His selfish ambitions in preaching had been surrendered, and he then received power by which to do his work for Christ.[6]

A "filling, a baptism or an anointing... and he then received power." Could this be anything other than a personal Pentecost? And it came sixteen years after he was saved and indwelt by the Holy Spirit. What

---

[4] Dorsett, p. 156.
[5] Wiersbe, p. 98.
[6] Wiersbe, p. 98.

followed Moody's Pentecost experience was what happened to the Apostle Peter. Moody began to preach and save thousands of souls.

In the summer of 1873, Moody and his musical accompanist, Ira Sankey, accepted the invitation to preach in the United Kingdom. Initially their meetings were sparsely attended and poorly received. Then, a young Baptist pastor, F. B. Meyer, endorsed Moody before a group of people where a few other pastors were in attendance. This small word of encouragement opened doors for Moody that led to a nation's revival.

> News of this revival spread across the border into Scotland. Unbelievers were being converted, backsliders were returning to the fold, Christians were revitalized and witnessing, and both joy and unity were evident among previously competing and warring ministers and laity of many sects. Many people said this had to be the work of the Holy Spirit. No men—and certainly no Americans—could effect such extraordinary circumstances on their own.[7]

Moody was an unlettered American, one of the least likely to succeed in this vainglorious empire and, therefore, a perfect choice to serve almighty God. He was a man like Gideon. He triumphed because God was with him. And he was chosen, like so many other heroes of the faith, so that people would ascribe the glory to God and not to Moody.

Moody was later asked to visit Edinburgh, the cultural and theological center of Scotland. From the night he first spoke to a somewhat doubtful audience, the Spirit of God was poured upon them, cutting across lines of class, gender, nationality, and age to convict people of their sins and turn their hearts to their only Savior. Wherever he went crowds gathered, and thousands were saved, as a skeptical world watched on in wonder. Moody became an international celebrity, the Billy Graham of his day.

SPIRITUAL GIFTS

Do we receive new spiritual gifts during this second stage of our walk with Christ?

Whatever spiritually empowering gift we need to achieve God's will can be given to us at any time on the Path. However, the gifts we received upon being indwelt by the Holy Spirit were designed to achieve His plan for us. Therefore, during this phase of Spirit-filling, and being anointed with power, we should focus on using these gifts with the expectation that God can make them even more powerful. As Paul told Timothy:

---

[7] Dorsett, p. 186.

> For this reason I remind you to *fan into flame the gift of God*, which is in you through the laying on of my hands, for God gave us *a spirit not of fear but of power* and love and self-control (2 Tim 1:6-7, emphasis added).

The second phase is about exercising God's power, His grace, to produce a bountiful harvest of good works for the glory of God.

THE SECRET TO WIELDING CHRIST'S POWER

How was God able to work so powerfully through Moody?

> Not everyone understood the secret of Moody's power, at least in the way he understood it. To him it was a simple matter of the sacred anointing that falls on the available man or woman who is willing to become less so that Jesus can become more.[8]

Moody was emptied of self and anointed with power. On this leg of our journey on the Path to Christlikeness our lives are sent in a new direction, namely, toward the final harvest, the culmination of God's plan for our lives. Paul took this idea of becoming "less so that Jesus can become more" to its ultimate conclusion:

> It is no longer I who live, but Christ who lives in me. And the life I now live in the flesh I live by faith in the Son of God, who loved me and gave himself for me (Gal 2:20).

God is not punishing His children in the wilderness; He is preparing them for their anointing. If we want to work mightily for God, then God must first work mightily on us. There are dead branches that need to be pruned, because they hinder our fruitfulness. And though it is painful to have them removed, it leads to a rich, eternal harvest.

We need not seek the wilderness, or the cross, to destroy our old nature. All we need do is make ourselves available to God. The Good Shepherd will lead us into the wilderness and—praise God—through it.

BUT MY LIFE SEEMS SO INSIGNIFICANT

Everyone has a destiny to fulfill and the only One who can measure its impact is God. Our goal is not to outdo anyone, but simply to run our own race. We make ourselves available to God, and we march forth in His power to accomplish the task He gives us.

We can be certain of this: We are inept judges of God. Yet our pride leads us to judge God all of the time. When we question the worth of our God-given task are we not judging the wisdom of God? Obviously, this is

---

[8] Dorsett, p. 242.

foolish for we cannot know how God will bless our work and make something that seems inconsequential an amazing expression of His glory.

To support this assertion, we return to the life of Moody. He was working in his uncle's shoe store when his Sunday school teacher, Edward Kimball, dropped by to see him. Kimball felt compelled to talk to Moody about how God loved him.

He later said, "I made what I afterwards felt was 'a very weak plea for Christ,' "[9] and it may have been. However, God can anoint our weak pleas with a power that cannot be withstood. As Peter's Pentecost sermon shows, it is not our charm or eloquence that saves; it is the power of God. His "very weak plea" resulted in Moody coming to a saving faith.

At the time, saving an unlettered teenager probably appeared to be a small accomplishment in the annals of evangelism, but Kimball's service as a Sunday school teacher achieved something that is still affecting the world. Several of Moody's enterprises—e.g., the Moody Bible Institute and the Moody Church—are still active.

If we are faithful over a little, God may make our "little" into something extraordinary. But even if He chooses not to do so, we can rest in this promise: If we are faithful in executing our small tasks, He will one day set us over much, and we will enter into the joy of our Master.

THE END OF IDOL WORSHIP

THE "GOD" OF THIS WORLD

This may be one of the most difficult sections in this book, because it can be so convicting. But if we seek to be Christlike, then our hearts need to be convicted so that we may topple one of the most powerful idols on the face of the earth.

Our modern world looks at idol worship and laughs. "We are too sophisticated to bow down to silly, wooden images of an animal or mythological god," they think. But God's second commandment, forbidding the worship of idols, does not have a shelf-life. It is a commandment deemed to be just as worthy of our attention as it was for any previous generation. And because it is no longer perceived to be a threat, idol worship is more dangerous than ever.

Of all of the idols vying for our affection, the most powerful one may be money. The world promotes the worship of this idol and countless millions bow down before it with unswerving devotion. When Jesus said

---

[9] Lt. Col. E. W. Halford, "The Sunday School Teacher Who Won the Country Boy," *Young Men*, Volume 40 (1914): 236.

you could not worship both God and money, He revealed how the idol of money was one of God's primary competitors for our hearts and minds.

Dethroning the money-god is essential to our spiritual progress and peace because, according to the diagnosis of Scripture, the cancer that may have metastasized the most extensively throughout our hearts and minds is the love of money:

> For the love of money is a root of all kinds of evils. It is through this craving that some have wandered away from the faith and pierced themselves with many pangs. (1 Tim 6:10)

Because of the seductive-corrupting power of money, Jesus allowed us no half-measures in our relationship with it. We cannot love God and be neutral toward money. We must love God and hate money. In the words of Jesus, "No one can serve two masters, for either he will hate the one and love the other, or he will be devoted to the one and despise the other. You cannot serve God and money" (Mt 6:24).

How do we balance living in the modern world, paying for a home, sending kids to college, and despising money?

We must change our relationship to money by viewing it in the same way we view the corrupting world system. We must remember that "the whole world lies in the power of the evil one" (1 Jn 5:19). It hates us. It is a kingdom that promotes sin and the love of money, and we should despise this world system and all that it values and promotes. Meanwhile, we can rest in the knowledge that "everyone who has been born of God overcomes the world" (1 Jn 5:4).

PENTECOST AND OUR RELATIONSHIP WITH MONEY

God's plan to dethrone the money-god, and change our relationship to money, involves our being filled with the Spirit. After the Spirit-filling at Pentecost the disciples relationship with money was transformed:

> Now the full number of those who believed were of one heart and soul, and no one said that any of the things that belonged to him was his own, but they had everything in common. ...There was not a needy person among them, for as many as were owners of lands or houses sold them and brought the proceeds of what was sold and laid it at the apostles' feet, and it was distributed to each as any had need (Ac 4:32, 34-35).

Some try to make this into an advertisement for socialism wherein everything is held in common, but generalizing the singular event of Pentecost makes little sense. Has there ever been a nation whose people were all Spirit-filled like these disciples?

No. Furthermore, the utopian socialist movements of the nineteenth century tried to establish communities based on principles like these and they all failed. Quickly.

The point is not to argue for or against socialism. What Pentecost illustrates is how the outpouring of the Holy Spirit changed the disciple's relationship with money. Instead of hoarding it for their own purposes, they celebrated giving it to meet the needs of others.

PROPORTIONAL GIVING

The Old Testament celebration of the Feast of Pentecost helps us see what our new relationship with money looks like:

> Then you shall keep the Feast of Weeks [also known as Pentecost] to the LORD your God with the tribute of a freewill offering from your hand, which *you shall give as the LORD your God blesses you* (Dt 16:10, emphasis and bracketed note added).

The Feast of Weeks does not say, "Give away your money until you are destitute." It says, "Give back to God a proportional gift of the blessings you've received from Him." Proportional giving is best known as tithing, or giving a tenth of all of your income to either the church you attend, or other Christian causes. It is proportional because 10% from $20,000, or $2,000, is much less than 10% from $200,000, or $20,000. The larger your blessing, the larger your gift.

Is ten percent the magic number? I remember asking a pastor about this and his answer was, "I think ten percent is the bare minimum." You could hear the air leaving my lungs. His words were like a fist in my stomach, because I was not tithing at the time. And I did not have any desire to do so for the following reasons:

> I needed the money. Ten percent was way too much. More than ten percent was insane. Churches are always trying to get my money so they could waste it. Besides, nowhere does Jesus say we need to tithe.

Regarding that last objection, Jesus said, "Woe to you, scribes and Pharisees, hypocrites! For *you tithe* mint and dill and cumin, and have neglected the weightier matters of the law: justice and mercy and faithfulness. *These you ought to have done*, without neglecting the others" (Mt 23:23, emphasis added). Far from disrespecting tithing, Jesus tells the hypocritical they ought to have tithed, but also should have honored God more powerfully by bearing the spiritual fruit of a just, merciful and faithful life.

As a faithful worshipper of money, I was ready to protect this idol at all costs. Proportional giving is almost impossible for a person who is in love with money. Jesus warned that it is easier for a camel to jump through the eye of a needle than for a rich man to enter God's Kingdom.

"Then who can be saved?" asked His disciples. Jesus answered, "This is impossible for man, but all things are possible for God." In other words, the Holy Spirit can change even the wealthy person's relationship with money.

Take Joseph of Arimathea. He is described as "a respected member of the council, who was also himself looking for the kingdom of God" (Mk 15:43). Elsewhere he appears as "a good and righteous man" (Lk 23:50), and "a rich man... who also was a disciple of Jesus" (Mt 27:57). Through the power of the Spirit, he was both rich and righteous, and this made him courageous enough to serve Jesus during a dangerous time. After the trial and crucifixion of Jesus, the apostles scattered to the four winds, but Joseph did not. He went to Pilate and asked for Jesus' body, to bury Him and seal the tomb. As "a respected member of the council" he risked ostracism, and condemnation from the high priest, but as a disciple of Jesus, he had a higher loyalty.

PUTTING GOD TO THE TEST

God invites us to do something with our wealth that He explicitly condemns elsewhere, namely, test Him in the area of tithing:

> Bring the full tithe into the storehouse, that there may be food in my house. And thereby put me to the test, says the LORD of hosts, if I will not open the windows of heaven for you and pour down for you a blessing until there is no more need (Mal 3:10).

This is a test worth taking because you cannot out-give God.

Lastly, do not think that by tithing you have fully uprooted this idol from your heart. It may still hold enormous power over your affections. We must never underestimate the power of sin's siren call.

WATCHMAN NEE AND MONEY

Watchman Nee was invited to speak at an evangelistic meeting in Chien-O, a town that was upriver about 150 miles. The fare by motorboat was $80 and he had $30. God impressed upon his heart the financial needs of another brother in Christ, and he responded to this by sending him $20.

> Next morning no one gave Watchman anything before he left, and as he crossed by ferry to the port with a mere $10 in his pocket he prayed in desperation, "Lord, I am not asking you for money; only to be taken to Chien-O!" Arrived at the pier he was accosted by the owner of a small steam launch who asked him, "Are you going to Yen-ping or Chien-O?" "To Chien-O," he replied.

"Come with me, then. I'll take you." "For how much?" "Only seven dollars." Amazed, he asked the reason as he carried his baggage on board. The boat, he learned, was under county charter, but the owner was free to earn a little extra by letting a seat to one passenger if it was not required by the hirers.[10]

The dire circumstances we may confront on the way toward God's provision of resources are not to punish us, but to wean us away from a faith in money, a faith in what we can touch, feel and see, and replace it with a faith in our invisible God.

PETER WALDO: THE RENUNCIATION OF THE WORLD

The Word of God does not command us to be poor, and the history of Christianity's greatest saints shows how one can serve God powerfully while living comfortably. However, some of those who have responded to the call to live a life of radical renunciation have changed the lives of many others, and in some cases the course of history.

Peter Waldo (c. 1140 AD – c. 1218 AD) was a rich merchant who was moved to adopt a lifestyle of voluntary poverty. He gave his property to his wife, distributed the remainder of his belongings as alms to the poor, and began to publicly preach how man cannot serve both God and Money. Many began to follow him and they were called Waldensians.

Waldo was a reformer long before the Reformation. In true Reformation fashion, he accused the pope of being the harlot in the Book of Revelation, and criticized the papacy for its lavish lifestyle. More importantly, he was the first to translate the Bible into a common tongue, thereby making it accessible to the common people who could not read Latin. Since the Waldensians believed one's life should conform to the Bible's teachings, it logically followed that Bibles should be made available to all so they would know what the Bible taught.

The Waldensians were radically different in a revitalizing way and people began to listen to these lay preachers and follow their teaching. The church responded in a predictable way. They persecuted them harshly, but were unable to destroy the movement. Ultimately, the Waldensians survived and became a part of the Reformed branch of the Protestant faith.

A lesson from Waldo's life is this: Our spiritual growth will be greatly accelerated once we live lives that despise money, a chief idol of this world, and joyfully give a portion of our wealth to support the work of the Kingdom. We mustn't just love God and ignore Money; we must love

---

[10] Angus Kinnear, *The Story of Watchman Nee: Against the Tide* (Wheaton, IL: Tyndale House Publishers, Inc., 1978), p. 85.

God and hate Money. Money is like an untrustworthy servant who needs to be kept in close quarters, under guard, and used when necessary.

Evidence of a new relationship with money is our ability to celebrate giving. This is why the Lord loves a cheerful giver. Such a person worships God and not Money.

I can imagine asking Peter Waldo at the end of his life, "Was giving away your wealth worth it? What do you have to show for it?" And then seeing him smile and reply, "You cannot out-give God. He is generous by nature and possesses all things. You cannot begin to imagine the riches that have poured into my life after I gave away my wealth to support the work of the Kingdom. I have the privilege of serving a loving God."

During every stage of the Path, from beginning to end, prayer occupies an important place in our discipleship training course. We've seen how prayer is closely associated with being Spirit-filled. This makes prayer a pathway to grace, the power of God. And when prayer is imbued with hope it is made more effective, because it aligns our prayers with the way Jesus taught us to pray.

EXPECTANT PRAYER

PRAYER FILLED WITH HOPE

Hope is a type of faith that lays hold of the future, because it expects, or believes, the future it envisions will be realized. And a hope-imbued faith is the attitude we should have when praying. It makes prayer expectant.

Faith is focused on the present. It says, "I believe God's Word is true." Hope is focused on the future and it adds, "And I believe His promises will be fulfilled."

Faith and hope are like two hands on the same keyboard playing different notes in the same song. We see this intermingling of hope and faith in the definition of faith found in Hebrews 11:1, "Now faith is the assurance of things hoped for, the conviction of things not seen."

We also find a remarkable intermixing of faith and hope in the Lord's instructions on prayer. He said, "Therefore I tell you, whatever you ask in prayer, believe that you have received it, and it will be yours" (Mk 11:24). Here we have faith and hope operating as one. But the expectancy of hope, that believes in a future realization of God's promises, is modified. It now believes that the future is here, right now, and spiritually speaking it is.

In the eternal mind of God, the future already exists because in His omniscience He knows what the future is. But in the sphere of time this future that is known by God must wait for His perfect timing before it is fulfilled on earth. It is guaranteed to happen, but it has not happened yet. However, in this fusion of faith and hope, we can believe the future is now, and we've already received what is promised.

Confused? Here is how this works out in our prayer life.

Faith looks at the Word of God and says, "I believe Jesus was telling us the truth when He said, 'If you then, who are evil, know how to give good gifts to your children, how much more will the heavenly Father give the Holy Spirit to those who ask him!' (Lk 11:13)." Faith also believes Paul's admonition, "And do not get drunk with wine, for that is debauchery, but be filled with the Spirit..." (Eph 5:18).

We now add ever-expectant hope to the mix and we pray, "Lord, since it is the Father's good pleasure to give the Holy Spirit to those who ask Him, and the Word tells us we should be filled with the Holy Spirit, I ask You, Father, to fill me with the Holy Spirit. Fill me to overflowing. And I know this prayer is answered, right now, because it is Your perfect will that this be so. May it make me a more effective servant. I pray this in the holy name of Jesus. Amen."

If you truly believe you've received what you've asked for, then what should follow receiving a great gift from God?

We should thank God for this gift:

> Dear heavenly Father, thank you for this gift of being filled with the Holy Spirit. My cup overflows. The riches in my treasure house make the wealthiest man on earth the humblest of paupers.

Your rational mind will bark, "Stop kidding yourself. I notice no change. Believe all you want, but you are deluding yourself."

To which faith and hope reply, "Dear reason, you live by sight. Comment all you want about the invisible world of Spirit, but I will not listen, for you are incapable of understanding that which you cannot see."

We must never despise the great gift of reason, but we must relegate its operation to its proper sphere. In the invisible, spiritual realm, reason is like a blind man leading the blind. When it comes to believing the promises of God and praying in a way that believes it has already received what was asked for, we must refuse to follow reason or we will be led into a ditch.

THE PROMISES OF GOD AND PRAYER

The message of faith and hope is, "Lay hold of the promises of God and believe that you've already received their fulfillment." It is an eternal perspective that cherishes the promises of God:

> His divine power has granted to us all things that pertain to life and godliness, through the knowledge of him who called us to his

own glory and excellence, by which he has granted to us *his precious and very great promises*, so that through them you may become partakers of the divine nature... (2 Pt 1:3-4, emphasis added).

We "become partakers of the divine nature" by faithfully believing the promises of God. This is another spiritual exercise leading to Christlikeness. So, with a heart filled with expectant faith, let us pray a few of the promises of God.

The Promise: "I can do all things through him who strengthens me" (Phil 4:13).

The Prayer: Father, I thank You for the strength to accomplish every task You have assigned me, no matter how impossible it may appear to be. I believe Your promises are fulfilled this moment in Jesus.

The Promise: "Many are the afflictions of the righteous, but the LORD delivers him out of them all" (Ps 34:19).

The Prayer: Father, whatever my faith test, whether it be health, relationships, finances, or fearing dire situations, I am thankful that, whatever it is, You will deliver me from it.

The Promise: "But the Lord is faithful. He will establish you and guard you against the evil one" (2 Thes 3:3).

The Prayer: Father, I thank you that I will remain established with You and the Kingdom of God, even if I am under spiritual attack from Satan, or the children of Satan. (In Chapter Six I will have much more to say about Satan and his children.)

The Promise: "You keep him in perfect peace whose mind is stayed on you, because he trusts in you" (Is 26:3).

The Prayer: Father, my rest, my peace, comes from trusting in You. And Your gift of faith, and the peace that comes with it, cannot be permanently taken away from me by anyone. Lord, keep my mind fixed on You, and may I always look to You, "the founder and perfecter of our faith" (Heb 12:2).

I recommend going through the promises of God and, exercising your hope in Christ, claim them as being fulfilled in Christ this very moment, for it is God's will that His promises be fulfilled.

SPIRIT-FILLED PRAYER

Our fallen nature instinctively looks to self for answers, but prayer exercises and develops spiritual muscles that incline our hearts and minds toward God. Therefore, we need to pray persistently to develop habits that lead to Christlikeness. Note, for example, the persistence of Jesus' prayer:

> In these days he went out to the mountain to pray, and *all night he continued in prayer* to God. And when day came, he called his disciples and chose from them twelve, whom he named apostles (Lk 6:12-13, emphasis added).

Talk about praying without ceasing! Given the poor condition of most people's prayer life, it is natural to ask, "Who could possibly pray all night?"

The answer is simple: When Jesus prayed, He was in the presence of God and it was like returning home. God was His oasis in the desert.

If our prayer life is weak, then perhaps we need to experience the presence of God through the Spirit-filling that inspires prayer. When we experience the Spirit-filling we are ushered into the presence of God and experience an unspeakable joy. Our prayer-life is imbued with power, and we begin to realize that the Spirit Himself is our willing prayer Partner:

> "The Spirit Himself," deeper down than our thoughts or feelings, "maketh intercession for us with groanings which cannot be uttered." When you cannot find words, when your words appear cold and feeble, just believe: The Holy Spirit is praying in me.[11]

The Holy Spirit will also lead us to pray for others, rather than just ourselves. As we progress along the Path, we will begin to feel burdened for others, as Edward Kimball felt burdened for Moody, and this prompting comes from the Holy Spirit. He is infusing our prayer life with the love of God that breaks us free from the bondage of self-centeredness.

If we are to love our neighbors as our self—the second commandment from Jesus—then we must pray for our neighbors as often, or more often, than for our self. And if we are to fulfill the first and greatest commandment—to love God with our entire being—then we must be filled with the Holy Spirit, for only through the power of God's Spirit can we love Him as completely as we are commanded to do.

BINDING AND LOOSING

The written Word of God was completed with John's Revelation, but that does not mean God has stopped giving us His words. Jesus told His disciples they would be delivered up to judges, but they need not worry about what they would say, "for I will give you a mouth and wisdom, which none of your adversaries will be able to withstand or contradict" (Lk 21:15).

---

[11] Andrew Murray, *The Ministry of Intercession: A Plea for More Prayer* (London: James Nisbet & Co. Limited, 1898), p. 120.

In Proverbs we read, "I will pour out my spirit to you; I will make my words known to you" (Pr 1:23), and this promise was fulfilled during the Holy Spirit baptism at Pentecost. God turned Christ's disciples into His mouthpieces, enabling them to share the gospel in a language they did not know.

The revelation of the words of God is a gift from our heavenly Father, communicated through the power of the Holy Spirit who is to lead us into all truth. And God's "word is truth" (Jn 17:17). For example, prior to Pentecost, the Father shared these words about Jesus with Peter, "You are the Christ, the Son of the living God" (Mt 16:16). And Jesus told Simon, after he said them, he was blessed, because his Father had revealed this to him. Peter was given the words that expressed the truth of God.

After Peter confessed that Jesus was the Christ, he was told that he was being given the keys to the Kingdom of God and that *whatever he bound on earth would be bound in heaven, and whatever he loosed on earth would be loosed in heaven* (see Mt 16:17-19).

When we speak the words God has given us, then what we bind on earth is bound in heaven, for God is bound by His words, and only by His words. He will share these world-changing words with those through whom He intends to work His will.

Imagine being armed with God's words. Can there be a greater blessing? Can we wield a mightier sword?

THE CHURCH AND PRAYER

This same binding-loosing formula appears again in the context of the church. In this case, Jesus offers a formula for reinstating, back into the fellowship of the church, a brother or sister who has sinned. Jesus then concludes:

> Truly, I say to you, whatever you bind on earth shall be bound in heaven, and whatever you loose on earth shall be loosed in heaven. Again I say to you, if two of you agree on earth about anything they ask, it will be done for them by my Father in heaven. For where two or three are gathered in my name, there am I among them (Mt 18:18-20).

This ability to fulfill the will of God on earth is given to us provided we are aligned with that will, or "are gathered in [Jesus'] name." God does not accommodate our whims, but He does use His servants to fulfill His plan of salvation through their speaking the eternal, world-transforming words He has given us.

When our prayers express God's will, then our words are reflections of His own and we are, through these prayers, moving closer to reflecting

Christ's image. For like Christ, we will be speaking the words of the Father: "And the word that you hear is not mine but the Father's who sent me" (Jn 14:24).

A POSSIBLE ILLUSTRATION OF BINDING AND LOOSING

How does this binding and loosing work? What does it look like?

Remember the story of D. L. Moody, and how Cooke and Hawxhurst were praying for him that he might *receive the power*? I believe God placed this burden on their hearts to pray for Moody, and then supplied them with the words that expressed His will. God chose Moody to be an evangelist, and to fulfill God's plan for him, he needed to "receive the power." Then what the prayers of Cooke, Hawxhurst, and later Moody, bound on earth was bound in heaven, and afterwards God fulfilled His will according to His perfect timing.

When we pray in Jesus' name—i.e., according to His nature and will—believing we have already received what we've asked for, are we not binding on earth what is bound in heaven? Is not the fulfillment of Christ's will inevitable? Once we express the desires of the Holy Spirit that provoke our prayer, heaven resoundingly shouts, "Amen!"

One day, when we stand before the throne of the Almighty, we will discover the role our prayers played in the drama unfolding on earth. May we realize what a great privilege God has given us in prayer, and may it motivate all of us to pray.

THE PRAYING CHURCH AND POWER

The visible church—made up of denominations, buildings, pastoral staffs, etc.—is a hot mess. It is often scandal-ridden, prioritizing politics over the gospel, cliquish and unwelcoming. But there is another church that is the Body of Christ, and it is the invisible church made up of the souls of the children of God. This glorious church is beloved by God and given great honor.

Paul understood how God planned to express His glory through this church, and how we would have a difficult time grasping the full implications of this. So, he used questions to help the readers of his letters comprehend the powerful role the church will play in the world:

> ...do you not know that the saints will judge the world? ...Do you not know that we are to judge angels? (1 Cor 6:2, 3)

Paul takes the role of the church even deeper into the unseen realm of Spirit. He writes about how the church will be used to reveal the wisdom of God to heavenly beings. Paul received the grace "to bring to light for everyone what is the plan of the mystery hidden for ages in God, who created all things, so that through the church the manifold wisdom of God might now be made known to the rulers and authorities in the heavenly places" (Eph 3:9-10).

How could a saved person reveal God's wisdom to a celestial being unless God gave him the words of wisdom that reveal it? He couldn't, and this is just one more indication that God gives His eternal words to His saints that they might pull down strongholds and speak the saving gospel to those who dwell in darkness. Though we are the sheep of Christ's pasture, once we speak the words of God we are able to roar like a Lion of Judah.

PRAYER GUIDELINES FROM SCRIPTURE

Jesus, and the apostles, believed prayer could lose its efficacy if done incorrectly. So, they gave us guidelines to follow that we might pray effectively. The following are some of them:

> Do not make a big show about prayer. It is between you and God.
> Sometimes the shortest prayers are the most impactful. The tax collector who prayed, "God be merciful to me, a sinner" (Lk 18:13), went home justified.
> Pray persistently and without ceasing.
> Ask for wisdom and the Holy Spirit.
> Address God as Father.
> Pray with others. When two or more gather in Jesus' name He is in their midst.
> Pray for others. And, as Paul did, pray for anyone to whom you are ministering.
> A prayer should end with "Amen." It is a Hebrew word meaning "truth," "certainty." This affirmation is akin to believing you have already received what you have prayed for. The word "amen" is an expression of hope, or expectant faith.

The use of the word "amen" usually comes at the end of a prayer. In the divine world of inversion, Jesus would often open His teaching with the word "amen." Whenever He says, "Verily, verily," or, "Truly, truly I say to you," He is saying, "Amen, amen I say to you." It was a way of announcing, "What you are about to hear is truth and certainty."

And with that we leave the world of prayer and move toward the final harvest, the seventh and final feast. But before we reach it, we encounter two more feasts, the Feast of Trumpets and the Day of Atonement. They will introduce us to a world where we will likely feel lost even while possessing a road map that tells us where we are.

STAGE THREE:

LOVE

5

THE FEAST OF TRUMPETS

THE FEAST OF TRUMPETS

Another name for the Feast of Trumpets is Rosh Hashanah which means "Head of the Year." It is the day marking the celebration of the Jewish New Year. But according to the Old Testament's numbering of months, it was the first day of the seventh month, and not the first day of the first month. So, what gives? Who puts New Year's Day in the middle of the year?

Rosh Hashanah was originally the first day of the first month, but as God inverted so much else, He also inverted time. He made what was the first month into the seventh, and what was the seventh into the first. Hence, we read the following about the month of Passover, "This month shall be for you the beginning of months. It shall be the first month of the year for you" (Ex 12:2).

The Feast of Trumpets marks the beginning of the sacred seventh month. The Day of Atonement, the sixth feast, was celebrated on the tenth day of this month. It was the holiest day of the year because it marked the only time a priest would enter the Holy of Holies, the innermost area of the Temple, where the presence of God dwelt.

THE SOUND OF A TRUMPET

A trumpet blast, or loud noises like thunder, or earthquakes, or rocks breaking apart, often precedes entering the presence of God. It is like a warning to prepare us for this ultimate humiliation. For to stand before God is to have our relative insignificance and frailty revealed to us in a way that literally flattens us with fear.

Just before Moses went up to the top of Mount Sinai to receive the Ten Commandments we read:

> On the morning of the third day there were thunders and lightnings and a thick cloud on the mountain *and a very loud trumpet blast*, so that all the people in the camp trembled. Then Moses brought the people out of the camp *to meet God*, and they took their stand at the foot of the mountain (Ex 19:16-17, emphasis added).

The typical response of someone who enters God's presence is to fall prostrate before Him, trembling with fear. All of creation—even the earth—trembles in the presence of God:

> Now Mount Sinai was wrapped in smoke because the LORD had descended on it in fire. The smoke of it went up like the smoke of a kiln, and the whole mountain trembled greatly. And *as the sound of the trumpet grew louder and louder*, Moses spoke, and God answered him in thunder (Ex 19:18-19, emphasis added).

This appearance of God, preceded by the sound of a trumpet growing ever louder, terrified the Israelites. They feared they might die if God spoke to them again. There is a method in all that God does in our lives, but the Israelites were unable to understand what He was doing, or why. Moses explained to them what God's purpose was: "Do not fear, for God has come to test you, that the fear of him may be before you, that you may not sin" (Ex 20:20). Like so much else on the Path to Christlikeness their faith was being tested to make it stronger. And the stronger our faith, the less likely we are to sin.

THE LIFE OF ELIJAH

Prior to entering the presence of God, Elijah went through an angel-led time of preparation. After lying down in the wilderness and praying for death, an angel visited Elijah, touched him and said, "Arise and eat." Waiting for Elijah was a cake and a jar of water which he ate and drank. He then lay down and rested and the angel repeated what he had done before. He touched Elijah again and said, " 'Arise and eat, for the journey is too great for you.' And he arose and ate and drank, and went in the strength of that food forty days and forty nights to Horeb, the mount of God" (1 Ki 19:7-8).[1]

---

[1] "Horeb" and "Sinai" are different names for the same mountain, according to many commentaries.

Elijah was being prepared to enter the presence of God. At the end of the forty-day period the LORD told Elijah, "Go out and stand on the mount before the LORD" (1 Ki 19:11). After he was commanded to stand "before the LORD," he experienced a strong wind that broke up rocks, followed by an earthquake and fire. One can imagine the noise this demonstration of God's power made, but God was not in any of these manifestations of His power. The next thing Elijah experienced was the sound of a gentle whisper. God was present in the gentlest expression of His all-powerful Word. Elijah wrapped his face in his cloak. His response suggests being overwhelmed by the presence of God and wanting to hide or disappear. God then told Elijah to anoint Elisha, the prophet who would replace him. With his work finished, and his sanctification complete, Elijah was ready for heaven's glory.

REVELATION

At the beginning of Revelation, John writes:

> I was in the Spirit on the Lord's day, and I heard behind me *a loud voice like a trumpet* saying, "Write what you see in a book and send it to the seven churches..." (Re 1:10-11, emphasis added).

When he turned around to see who was speaking he saw "one like a son of man... and his face was like the sun shining at full strength" (Re 1:13,16). After hearing a trumpet-like sound, John entered the presence of God the Son, and he "fell at his feet as though dead" (Re 1:17). The presence of God empties us of self to the point where we do not have the strength or courage to stand. If John, the beloved of Jesus, is so affected by Jesus, then imagine how His presence might affect us.

To be in the presence of God is an experience reserved for the saints who come as close as possible to understanding the love of God. Yes, it is initially humbling, but ultimately ennobling. After God empties us of self, He always lifts us up.

Finally, the blast of a trumpet, and the largest earthquake in history, will precede the Second Coming of Christ. This will not merely mark a New Year, but the beginning of a new historical era called the Millennium. When Jesus returns, all of the inhabitants of the earth will be in the presence of God, and they will tremble with fear. It is called "the last trumpet," because there will be no need to sound the trumpet again. For Jesus is returning to stay, and those who belong to Him will be in the presence of God forever.

UNDERSTANDING THE LOVE OF GOD

When Jesus was asked, "Which is the great commandment in the law?" He said it was to love God with your entire being and the second commandment was like it, namely, to love your neighbor as yourself. Then, just before His crucifixion, He gave us what He called "my commandment":

> This is my commandment, that you love one another as I have loved you. Greater love has no one than this, that someone lay down his life for his friends (Jn 15:12-13).

His personal commandment to us was to love one another with the most radical degree of love possible, a love willing to go to the cross for someone else. After saying this, Jesus would be arrested a few hours later, tried and sentenced to death on a cross. He would be laying down His life for His friends. The cross is, therefore, the greatest expression of love.

We cannot imagine the infinite depths and dimensions of Christ's love, but we should try. God wants us to try. And to enable us to understand His love, and receive the blessings this knowledge confers, He makes us undergo the most radical surgery yet. This operation is reserved for the spiritually mature. A babe in Christ could not endure it, and were it not for the intervention of the grace of God, no one could endure it.

The Feast of Trumpets warns us that the Day of Atonement is approaching. After the trumpet sounds, we have ten days to prepare ourselves for entering the presence of God. Like the number seven, ten is a number of completion and perfection. In other words, God's timing will ensure we are fully prepared for this experience. And we will need such preparation, because the Day of Atonement introduces us to one of the Path's most perplexing places. I call it the wilderness of the righteous.

6

THE DAY OF ATONEMENT

ENTERING THE PRESENCE OF GOD

THE DAY OF ATONEMENT

The Day of Atonement is the only feast that is a fast. Instead of eating the "bread of affliction," our diet is now nothing but "affliction." Perhaps that is why it is never referred to as the "Feast" of Atonement. Instead, it was called a "Day," and unlike most feasts, it was designed to empty us:

> It shall be for you a time of holy convocation, *and you shall afflict yourselves* and present a food offering to the LORD. ...For *whoever is not afflicted on that very day shall be cut off from his people*. ...It shall be to you a Sabbath of solemn rest, and *you shall afflict yourselves* (Le 23:27, 29, 32, emphasis added).

During the Day of Atonement, a priest offered sacrifices to atone for both his sins and the sins of Israel. This links this feast unmistakably to the crucifixion, where our sins are forgiven. As the author of Hebrews noted:

> For Christ has entered, not into holy places made with hands, which are copies of the true things, but into heaven itself.... Nor was it to offer himself repeatedly, as the high priest enters the holy places every year with blood not his own.... But as it is, he has appeared once for all at the end of the ages to put away sin by the sacrifice of himself (Heb 9:24, 25, 26).

The imagery is clear. Fasting, the crucifixion, entering the presence of God, atoning for our sin... we are once again being operated on by the cross, only this time it is like being nailed to it.

THE TRIAL OF GOD-FORSAKENNESS

In the wilderness of the righteous we undergo the most painful procedure of our spiritual lives; and then, when we turn to God, He is not there. We begin to feel what Jesus felt on the cross and join Him in saying, "My God, my God, why have you forsaken me?" (Mt 27:46) It is the most confusing training we will undergo in this school of faith. Some of the most revered saints felt lost during this part of the Path, and several even expressed a white-hot anger toward God.

To feel forsaken by God, and maintain one's faith, is no small matter. It is the ultimate faith test. We return to Luther's theology of the cross:

> The most severe trial comes upon a person when he believes he has been forsaken and rejected by God.
> ...*This is then the highest degree of faith*, to cling to the grace of God even in the trial of God-forsakenness. This faith is no trifle; it is nothing less than a struggle with God against God.[1]

Luther's description recalls the image of Jacob wrestling with God and desperately clinging to Him. But being forsaken by God has another layer of suffering and that is being abandoned to Satan's torment. God will lower our hedge of protection to allow this, and do not think your right standing with God will protect you from this assault. For, as the following stories illustrate, the likelihood that you will be handed over to Satan for testing increases as you become more Christlike.

JOB VS. SATAN

The story of Job indicates how he was not only a righteous man, he was perhaps the most righteous man on earth:

> And the LORD said to Satan, "Have you considered my servant Job, that *there is none like him on the earth, a blameless and upright man,* who fears God and turns away from evil?" (Job 1:8, emphasis mine)

Job was reflecting God's image on earth. He was "blameless and upright." So why would God direct Satan's violent hatred toward him by asking, "Have you considered my servant Job?" That is a question that will take some time to answer.

Once Satan's attention was directed toward Job, he pointed out that Job had a hedge of protection around his family, property, and himself. But if God lowered this hedge, Satan added, and allowed him to destroy

---

[1] Loewenich, pp.136-137. Emphasis added.

all this, Job would curse God to His face. God's response was to lower the hedge.

Satan then kills Job's children and takes away his wealth. Job then makes his poetic confession of faith that reveals how he knew who took his wealth away. It wasn't Satan; it was God: "The LORD gave, and the LORD has taken away; blessed be the name of the LORD" (Job 1:21).

In this wilderness of the righteous we will find the most acute degrees of pain and anguish, and it can come in unrelenting waves. At this moment, Job's position with God was still rock solid. But God directed Satan's attention again toward Job and allowed Satan to attack a second time. This resulted in Job being covered from head to toe with boils.

Imagine experiencing agonizing pain from the slightest movement every moment of the day. At this point Job reached his limit, or so he probably thought. We read:

> After this Job opened his mouth and cursed the day of his birth. And Job said: "Let the day perish on which I was born..." (Job 3:1–3).

There were additional waves of torment heading for the shores of Job's soul. His wife told him to curse God and die. And his friends, who came to comfort him, were devoid of compassion. They told him he must have sinned to receive such a harsh judgment from God. But the mightiest wave of affliction was yet to come: Entering the presence of God.

As with Elijah, there is no explicit statement telling us that Job suffered from a pride problem, or that his many blessings from God made him conceited, but we can infer this from his behavior, and what he says in response to these trials. He believed what God was doing was wrong and he could prove it. He would justify himself, even if this came at God's expense.

He prayed that God would meet him so that he could argue his case face-to-face: "Though he slay me, I will hope in him; yet I will argue my ways to his face" (Job 13:15). And like a good lawyer, he was ready to defend himself, "Behold, I have prepared my case; I know that I shall be in the right" (Job 13:18).

If Job is in the right, then God must be in the wrong. To justify yourself at the expense of God is to be both proud and foolish. How can we know more about our situation than God? And yet what keeps Job from being cut off from God, despite his arrogant pride, is his unwavering faith. Though God may destroy him, Job said, he will still hope in Him. He later added, "For I know that my Redeemer lives, and at the last he will stand upon the earth" (Job 19:25).

But the trial of God-forsakeness is not over for Job. He had lost his family, wealth, health, and his friends were an additional source of torment, but he still had a proud heart. On the Path this is like a spiritually fatal malignancy that must be excised for our soul's sake.

JOB VS. GOD

The cross's mission in this final stage is to empty us completely of self. Job might have thought he could endure no more, but God had a final test in store for him: Being in His presence. This is not sweet communion with God, like Moody experienced during his personal Pentecost. No, this is standing before an awesome and fear-inspiring God whose mission is to destroy whatever is left of our old nature. It is confronting a God who demands we tell Him our name, admitting defeat and unconditionally surrendering ourselves to His care.

When God confronts Job, He does not try to comfort him. Instead, He focuses on making Job feel how insignificant his understanding is when compared to God's knowledge of all things:

> Where were you when I laid the foundation of the earth? Tell me, if you have understanding. Who determined its measurements— surely you know! (Job 38:4-5)

In other words, "Job, how can you possibly think you are in the right and I am in the wrong, when I know all things and you know next to nothing?" Job's suffering failed to humble him, but God would not fail.

Job finally responds to God's many questions by saying, "I had heard of you by the hearing of the ear, but now my eye sees you; therefore I despise myself, and repent in dust and ashes" (Job 42:5-6). In God's presence our imperfection stands in contrast to His perfection. God wants us to experience this complete humiliation, because it excises the last remnants of our old nature until all that remains is Christ.

Thankfully, this is not the end of the story. The purpose of the soul-reshaping wilderness of the righteous is not to curse, but to bless:

> And the LORD restored the fortunes of Job, when he had prayed for his friends. And the LORD gave Job twice as much as he had before. ...And the LORD blessed the latter days of Job more than his beginning (Job 42:10, 12).

While in the wilderness, we would do well to remind ourselves that God loves us, and He knows what He is doing. And just as He made the founder of our "salvation perfect through suffering" (Heb 2:10), He makes us complete through suffering as well.

PETER VS. SATAN

Job wasn't the only esteemed saint who Satan was allowed to attack. The Apostle Peter was another who experienced this. Jesus told Peter, "Simon, Simon, behold, Satan demanded to have you, that he might sift you like wheat…" (Lk 22:31).

Of all the apostles, Peter was the one most full of self. Therefore, Jesus did not deny Satan's request. But He did pray that Peter's faith would not fail, and that he would strengthen his brothers once he returned to their fellowship. This suggests this experience would ultimately make him stronger and more capable of serving God than those who did not experience this trial. As Luther said, a faith that survives the trial of God-forsakenness is no trifle. This ordeal emptied Peter of self and prepared him to be filled with the Holy Spirit and lead the church in Jerusalem.

PAUL VS. SATAN

Earlier we saw Paul being tormented by a messenger of Satan after receiving visions of paradise, and hearing things so profound he was not allowed to share them. The unbearable nature of this torment is revealed by Paul's praying three times for this thorn in his flesh to be removed. This mirrored Jesus' anguished prayer, just before His crucifixion, wherein He asked God three times to take the cup of His wrath away.

Like Peter, Paul was being tested. His independence was being attacked so that he might cultivate an even deeper Christ-dependence. The apostles, Peter and Paul, were afflicted by Satan and what was the result? They became the most fruitful leaders of the church. They might be the most blessed of the apostles, because they were also the most emptied.

THE SERPENT'S WAR AGAINST HUMANITY

You may be wondering, "What do attacks by Satan have to do with me?"

Everything. You and I are in a war against Satan and his children. As Paul wrote:

> Put on the whole armor of God, that you may be able to stand *against the schemes of the devil.* For we do not wrestle against flesh and blood, but against the rulers, against the authorities, *against the cosmic powers* over this present darkness, *against the spiritual forces of evil in the heavenly places* (Eph 6:11-12; emphasis added).

This cosmic war is ultimately being waged on earth, and it began in the Garden of Eden. After Satan deceived Eve, God revealed how there is enmity between the offspring of the serpent and the offspring of the woman (see Gen 3:15). Yes, there are children of Satan, and we need to become familiar with them, and their enmity toward us, or we will fail to understand what is happening to the world right now, and possibly to us. God might lower our hedge of protection and allow the children of Satan to torment us so that we might become leaders within the invisible church in these last days. That said, our prayer must always be, "And lead us not into temptation, but deliver us from the evil one" (Mt 6:13).[2]

TWO FATHERS, TWO LINEAGES

In Matthew's Parable of the Weeds, there are two spiritual lineages. They are called "the sons of the evil one" and "the sons of the kingdom" (see Mt 13:38). According to this parable, God is the Father of the sons of the kingdom, and Satan is the father of the sons of the evil one.

The two different lineages can be identified by their behaviors. As the Apostle John put it, "By this it is evident who are the children of God, and who are the children of the devil: whoever does not practice righteousness is not of God, nor is the one who does not love his brother" (1 Jn 3:10). John not only taught us there are two spiritual lineages, he also taught us how to tell them apart.

Understanding this conflict helps us understand some of Jesus' commands like, "Love your enemies." Though these children of the evil one hate us, we must love and pray for them, because we were once fallen members of their family. If we were not born again, through the power of God, we would still be their kith and kin. Prior to salvation, we were once dominated by the lusts of the flesh, the temptations of the world, and to varying degrees, the influence of Satan, just as they are now. Those who are still imprisoned in this world need to be liberated, like we were, and that is why we must be willing to continually pray for their salvation.

Our war against Satan and his children is not with weapons that cripple and kill. That is how they fight. Instead, we prosecute our war the way Jesus did, through self-sacrificing love and wielding His saving Word, the gospel.

WHAT IS THE PURPOSE OF THIS WAR?

The battle rages on, despite our best efforts to be peacemakers. Until our enemies are born again, their hatred will not let them rest. And as they try to destroy us, cancel us, or harass us until we can take no more, God anoints our willingness to suffer for our faith in such a way that it opens the eyes of many of those who are witnessing this.

Imagine watching innocent people calmly marching to their unjust deaths instead of abjuring Christ. Those who lived in pagan Rome saw

---

[2] *The New International Version* (2011). Zondervan.

this and knew these persecuted Christians possessed something real, something worth dying for, and something they now wanted. Instead of thinning the ranks of the church, the martyring of Christians expanded its ranks. For the testimony of faith in the face of persecution and death can liberate Satan's slaves.

Tertullian (c. 160 – c. 240 AD) noted "the oftener we are mowed down by you, the more in number we grow; the blood of Christians is seed." As the children of the devil killed each innocent follower of Christ, several more Christians were added to the church. The God who powerfully anoints the cross of Christ, also anoints our sacrifice.

Christians appear to be over-matched in this great battle of the end times. It is a war that will only grow more intense as this final period nears its end. It will require courage and faith in the God who has armed us with the sword of the Spirit, the Word of God, the greatest power in the universe. For by God's Word the universe was created. Our faithless foe cannot hold this sword, but in the hands of believers it is inverting our fallen world, turning what is upside-down, right-side-up.

The wilderness of the righteous, of being forsaken by God, takes God's saints to the edge of the abyss. It is a mystery of the cross; and only the cross can explain it.

THE MYSTERY OF THE CROSS

FAITH AND UNDERSTANDING

To understand why we are sent into the wilderness of the righteous we must first establish the association that exists between faith, understanding and love, and the impact this has on becoming Christlike.

Faith and understanding are closely associated with one another in Luke and Matthew's versions of the Parable of the Sower. In Luke a person hears the Word and, before he can *believe* it and be saved, the devil snatches it away:

> The ones along the path are those who have heard; then the devil comes and takes away the word from their hearts, so that they may not *believe and be saved* (Lk 8:12, emphasis added).

Luke emphasizes believing, or a saving *faith*, but in Matthew a person hears the Word and, before he *understands* it, the devil snatches it away:

> When anyone hears the word of the kingdom and *does not understand it*, the evil one comes and snatches away what has been sown in his heart. This is what was sown along the path. ...As for what was sown on good soil, this is *the one who*

> *hears the word and understands it. He indeed bears fruit* and yields, in one case a hundredfold, in another sixty, and in another thirty" (Mt 13:19, 23, emphasis added).

Our fruitful works do not save us, but our saving faith, that enables us to understand the Word of God, produces a rich harvest of fruitful works.

UNDERSTANDING LOVE'S DIMENSIONS

To become Christlike, we must be emptied of self and filled with the Holy Spirit, and nothing else:

> …that you, being rooted and grounded in love, may have strength to *comprehend* with all the saints what is the breadth and length and height and depth, and to *know* the love of Christ that surpasses knowledge, that you may be *filled with all the fullness of God* (Eph 3:17-19, emphasis added).

To "comprehend," or understand, the dimensions of Christ's love is to be "filled with all the fullness of God." Jesus told us that the greatest expression of love was laying down one's life for His friends, which He did for us on the cross. So, if we are to understand the heights and depths of Christ's love, then we must understand the love represented by the cross.

However, as the above verse states, understanding this love "surpasses knowledge." The head cannot acquire it. It must be obtained by the heart and this illumination occurs through our experiencing the cross. And just as Jesus felt what it was like to be forsaken by God while on the cross, so do we.

CRUCIFIED WITH JESUS

The wilderness of the righteous is a reenactment of the crucifixion. We feel forsaken by God just like Jesus did. Jesus was also tormented by Satan during the crucifixion. When the religious leaders came to arrest Jesus and then crucify Him, He told them, "But this is your hour, and the power of darkness" (Lk 22:53).

Satan, the power of darkness, tempted Jesus in the wilderness, and then "left him until an opportune time" (Lk 4:13). That opportune time was during the crucifixion when the power of darkness reigned. Once Jesus took upon Himself the sins of the world, He became sin, was forsaken by God, and subject to the torment of Satan. And just as Satan tormented Jesus, he also torments us when we experience the cross.

The wilderness of the righteous is disorienting. Like Job, we are unable to understand what is happening to us or why it is happening. Our confusion is amplified by the way our souls feel a level of pain we've never experienced before. We pray and hope with all of our might that this painful process will end, but it doesn't. That is because we must experience the suffering of the crucifixion to the degree we are able. And so as not to diminish Jesus' sacrifice, our level of suffering will never compare to that which our Lord experienced.

Until we suffer the crucifixion, within our limitations, we have a superficial understanding of the words, "For *God so loved the world*, that he gave his only Son, that whoever believes in him should not perish but have eternal life" (Jn 3:16, emphasis added). But when we experience a miniscule sampling of what Jesus suffered for us, and how painful it is, we begin to understand the depth of His love for us. This understanding fortifies our faith, because we now know if Christ loves us so deeply that He would suffer this for us, then He will only do what is best for us.

Once we have been emptied of self by the wilderness of the righteous, we are ready to receive God's blessing and be "filled with all of the fullness of God." We will now see how this process unfolded in the life of C. S. Lewis.

C. S. LEWIS IN THE WILDERNESS

THE FEAR-INSPIRING CROSS

Prior to entering the wilderness of the righteous, C. S. Lewis sensed how experiencing the cross was not for the fainthearted:

> Does God then forsake just those who serve him best? Well, He who served Him best of all said, near His tortured death, 'Why hast thou forsaken me?' When God becomes man, that Man, of all others, is least comforted by God, at His greatest need. There is a mystery here which, even if I had the power, I might not have the courage to explore. Meanwhile, little people like you and me, if our prayers are sometimes granted, beyond all hope and probability, had better not draw hasty conclusions to our own advantage. If we were stronger, we might be less tenderly treated. If we were braver, we might be sent, with far less help, to defend far more desperate posts in the great battle.[3]

Lewis was face-to-face with the mystery of the cross and it intimidated him. This revealed his wisdom, not his cowardice. For strength and bravery may equip us for the "desperate posts in the great battle," but the cross requires more than this. It takes a supernatural degree of trust, a faith

---

[3] C.S. Lewis, *The Essential C.S. Lewis*, ed. Lyle Dorsett (NY: Touchstone, 1996), p. 382.

strengthened by the prayers of Jesus, to enable us to emerge intact and better for it.

LEWIS AND THE TRIAL OF GOD-FORSAKENESS

After penning such Christian classics as *Mere Christianity,* and *The Chronicles of Narnia*, C. S. Lewis suffered the loss of his wife Joy. He was sixty-one years old at the time of her death and would die a short three years later. His spiritual maturity, however, was no match for this wilderness of the righteous. No man's is. And his grief turned into a white-hot anger against God. He wrote:

> Eventually I must face the question in plain language. What reason have we, except our own desperate wishes, to believe that God is, by any standard we can conceive, "good?" Doesn't all the prima facie evidence suggest exactly the opposite? What have we to set against it?
>
> We set Christ against it, but how if He were mistaken? Almost His last words may have a perfectly clear meaning. He had found that the Being He called Father was horribly and infinitely different from what He had supposed. The trap, so long and carefully prepared and so subtly baited, was at last sprung, on the cross. The vile practical joke had succeeded.[4]

His equating the crucifixion to a "carefully prepared" trap and a "vile practical joke" is stunning enough, but the pain he experienced while in this wilderness produced more shrieks of agony:

> What chokes every prayer and hope is the memory of all the prayers H. [i.e., his wife, Joy Lewis] and I offered and all the false hopes we had. Not hopes raised merely by our own wishful thinking; hopes encouraged, even forced upon us, by false diagnoses, by x-ray photographs, by strange remissions, by one temporary recovery that might have ranked as a miracle. Step by step we were 'led up the garden path.' Time after time, when He seemed most gracious He was really preparing for the next torture.[5]

Read, once more, that last sentence in the above quote, for it tells us how the trial of God-forsakeness feels. It feels like we are being water-boarded, or stretched on the rack. And when he refers to "the next torture," we are reminded of the way Job experienced affliction in wave after wave.

---

[4] Clive Staples Lewis, *A Grief Observed* (New York: HarperOne, 1989), p. 42.

[5] Clive Staples Lewis, *A Grief Observed*, pp. 42-43. My bracketed note.

His soul-pain was so intense it made him wonder if God is a "Cosmic Sadist," an "Eternal Vivisector." That's a strong mischaracterization of God, but did not Job do the same thing as he wondered lost in this alien terrain? Job's anger made him wonder if God was morally indifferent:

> When disaster brings sudden death, he mocks at the calamity of the innocent. The earth is given into the hand of the wicked; he covers the faces of its judges— if it is not he, who then is it? (Job 9:23-24)

Job realized that God is sovereign over human history, and when he tried to determine the cause of his suffering, or how wickedness thrives on earth, he concluded, "My God, You are responsible for this! For if it is not You, then who is it?" In this wilderness our world seems upside down and so does our God.

Finally, Lewis's cries of pain were written and edited. He could have softened the edges of his rant in the rewriting process, but he didn't. He felt what he experienced was worth sharing with others, and he was right. He went through the crucible of God's healing love and he was able to reveal how it can make one feel completely unhinged and lost until the operation is over.

THE PATH TO CHRISTLIKENESS

When A. N. Wilson wrote his biography of C.S. Lewis he was no friend of the faith. Some years later he wrote about how he was invited to exchange his views with Victor Stock, the rector of St. Mary-le-Bow in the City of London:

> Memory says that while Father Stock was asking me about Lewis, I began to "testify," denouncing Lewis's muscular defence of religious belief.
> ... I can remember almost yelling that reading C S Lewis's *Mere Christianity* made me a non-believer—not just in Lewis's version of Christianity, but in Christianity itself.[6]

Yet this same A. N. Wilson honestly noted in his biography about Lewis, how he experienced something akin to sanctification at the end of his life:

> If we ignore the kind of man Lewis was, in our anxiety to dismiss him as a fraud or canonize him as a plaster saint, we miss the unmistakable and remarkable evidence of something like

---

[6] A.N. Wilson, "Why I believe again," New Statesman, 2 Apr 2009. Wilson, praise God, returned to the faith. This is the link to the article: https://www.newstatesman.com/religion/2009/04/conversion-experience-atheism.

sanctification which occurred in him towards the end of his days. The suffering which smashed him up and made him so vulnerable did not destroy his faith.

...Like many (most?) religious people, Lewis was profoundly afraid of death. ...Physical extinction was a perpetual nightmare to him and, whatever his theological convictions and hopes, he was unable, before his wife's death, to reconcile himself to the transition which death must inevitably entail.

Towards the end, this changed. It was not that he developed a death wish: his hold on life was as vigorous as ever. But he became altogether more accepting of the cards that were being dealt to him. The last years at Cambridge were happy ones.[7]

Lewis's last days remind me of Job's: "And the LORD blessed the latter days of Job more than his beginning." As this snapshot of the end of Lewis's life shows, God knew what He was doing. The divine hand that holds the pruning shears does not hesitate when it is cutting away all that hinders our spiritual fruitfulness. Lewis survived the procedure and was better for it. This final application of the cross makes us whole, "perfect through suffering," just as it did C. S. Lewis.

His intense suffering in the sphere of time increased his fruitfulness, his ability to rest, and will yield eternal rewards. It was Paul who put our sufferings in perspective, "For I consider that the sufferings of this present time are not worth comparing with the glory that is to be revealed to us" (Rom 8:18).

Like all sinners, I was at the foot of the cross when I was saved. As I've walked down sanctification's Path, suffering many painful periods of discipline, I find I am still at the foot of the cross. I doubt I will ever leave its shadow. I've not enjoyed these extended stays in the wilderness, but I know our Lord is the pinnacle of wisdom. Sadly, I must have needed this to humble my proud, self-centered soul and I am certain the Lord's discipline will be applied as often as needed to keep me from becoming conceited. And the same holds true for you, and for every fallen person throughout history.

We are now headed toward the final harvesting of fruit, not grain. Therefore, I will end this last stage on the Path to Christlikeness with vignettes of God's saints who produced spiritual fruit like faith, hope and love in their lives. They lived meaningful lives that, far from being restless, expressed deep satisfaction and peace.

---

[7] A. N. Wilson, *C. S. Lewis: A Biography* (New York: W. W. Norton and Co., 1990), pp. 292, 293.

7

THE FEAST OF INGATHERING

THE SPIRITUAL FRUIT OF FAITH

THE FEAST OF INGATHERING

Being turned inside out is not fun, but by the grace of God, we've made it to the final celebration: The Feast of Ingathering. During this feast the Israelites would celebrate the last harvest of the year, harvesting fruit like dates, olives, figs and pomegranates.

It is the leitmotif that is repeated throughout the Path to Christlikeness. At every stage of our journey, our destiny is to bear fruit to the glory of God. As Jesus said:

> I am the vine; you are the branches. Whoever abides in me and I in him, he it is that bears much fruit, for apart from me you can do nothing. … By this my Father is glorified, that you bear much fruit and so prove to be my disciples (Jn 15:5, 8).

But unlike the feast celebrated by the Israelites long ago, we bear spiritual fruit. There are many different types of fruit, according to Scripture, but we will focus on three of them: Faith, hope, and love.

THE VISION OF FAITH

When a worshipper of God makes himself available, he will receive an assignment. For Jeremiah Lanphier this task was communicated by a passing thought, "God wants the people to pray." The insistence of this thought grew until he could no longer ignore it. Then, as he attended to this assignment, he saw a way to satisfy God's will, and did so.

God enabled Charles Colson to see the needs of prisoners by making him one. His Prison Ministries then became the world's largest organization ministering to the incarcerated and their families.

As the above indicates, the assignment we receive may be communicated in different ways, but it is faith, the sensory organ of the soul, that enables us to perceive what the task is. For faith has the ability to apprehend the invisible. It "is the assurance of things hoped for, the conviction of things not seen" (Heb 11:1).

The author of Hebrews continued by noting the lives of several champions of the faith and added, "These all died in faith, not having received the things promised, but *having seen them* and greeted them *from afar...*" (Heb 11:13, emphasis added).

Faith receives a vision from God that is often fuzzy at first; we see it from afar. But, according to God's timing, it comes into focus and compels us to move. We then march down this path of service even when we have no idea where it is leading. We may not know how we can accomplish the task, but continue on because we have this sense that God can, and our heart is burdened by His Spirit to complete the assignment.

The lives of many saints illustrate this process and we will look at two of them.

WORLD VISION

God uses imperfect people, like you and me, to accomplish His work in this world. Bob Pierce was one of these flawed servants whose eyes of faith saw a need that compelled him to act.

In the late 1940s, Pierce was a Youth for Christ evangelist sharing the gospel to the attendees of a mission school for girls. He told them to go home and tell their parents that they were now going to follow Jesus. The next day a missionary carried a little girl whose back was bleeding from the beating she received. He placed the girl in Bob's arms and delivered this message: "You told this poor little girl to do that. Now you take care of her. If you think you can come in here, preach, and not do anything, you are wrong."[1]

Being held accountable is a bracing experience. Pierce could see the unintended consequences of his actions and it shook him. He emptied his pockets of the five dollars he had to provide for the little girl and promised to keep sending the same amount each month to provide for her needs.

This experience enabled Pierce to see what only the eyes of faith can see. He now saw how missionaries were unable to meet many of the basic

---

[1] Todd Temple, Kim Twitchell, *People Who Shaped the Church* (Wheaton, Illinois: Tyndale House Publishers, Inc., 2000), p. 252.

needs of the people they served. And then he saw a way to address this problem. He would get others to see what the little girl enabled him to see.

To do this he went to China with a video camera and began to film the faces of the poor. He then showed this film to churches and asked people to adopt one of the children by donating a small amount each month to help sustain them. His actions to help a little girl became the initial business plan behind World Vision, an organization he founded, and it became the largest Christian relief and development agency in the world.

However, there is a sad side to this story. His work on behalf of others came at the expense of his own family. He was gone much of the time. He failed to divide his love for the poor and for his family in a balanced way. It led to a divorce, bitter children, and might even have contributed to the tragic decision of one of his daughters to commit suicide.

There can be little doubt his words and actions caused his daughters great suffering. One of them wrote about how he told her, "Doesn't Luke 14:26 say we must hate mother and father, wife and children to be Christ's disciple? ... Well that's what I'm doing."[2]

Was he unbalanced? Yes. Was he an imperfect man who failed his family in many ways? Unquestionably. But did God use him mightily? Yes, and the Bob Pierces of the world should give us hope. As imperfect as he was, and we are, we can still serve God powerfully.

Bob retired from World Vision in 1967. The organization he founded was no longer his, and he lost his family as well. He was walking in the wilderness of the righteous, and when he graduated from this desert school God gave him another assignment. He founded Samaritan's Purse in 1970, another international relief organization that is now run by his friend, Franklin Graham, the son of Billy Graham.

Bob Pierce, even with his many failings, was a man of great faith. For he saw a need that was invisible to many others, was moved by it, and through the grace of God was able to discharge his duty and bear a rich harvest of spiritual fruit.

LIVING THE VISION

Anjeze Gonxhe Bojaxhiu felt the call to lead a life dedicated to Jesus at the age of twelve. At the age of eighteen she joined the Sisters of Loreto, adopted the name Teresa, and left for India to serve as a teacher. It would be her profession for the next twenty years.

After a while, Calcutta's in-your-face poverty began to disturb her deeply, and these feelings could not be quieted. Her eyes of faith were starting to focus on her new calling from God. Then, while traveling by

---

[2] Temple, Twitchell, p. 255.

train to an annual retreat, she felt her "call within the call." Sister Teresa left her convent to live amongst the poorest of the poor and minister to them. We now know her by the name Mother Teresa.

THE CROSS TESTS OUR FAITH

Mother Teresa needed faith to leave the "comfort" and safety of the convent and follow her calling, for she had no income and had to beg for food to live. She became like the people she was serving and experienced the desperate challenges of poverty.

Everyone is subjected to the cross and the first year of Mother Teresa's journey was more difficult than she ever thought it would be. The temptation to return to the convent was so strong she believed it came from the devil. As the cross prepared her for her life's work, it is likely Satan did torment her in this wilderness of the righteous. Her faith was certainly tested.

But she overcame these trials and, according to her, the secret for success was simple: She prayed. She looked to God and depended on Him. From start to finish, we who are on the Path to Christlikeness look to Jesus, receive His favor, and express it by loving God and others.

Mother Teresa believed God's judgment would not ask her how many good things she did in this life, but would ask her how much love she put into what she did. Her believing this is not surprising since her ministry was one of self-sacrificial love for the unloved, the lepers, the homeless, the blind, the crippled and the naked.

She founded the Missionaries of Charity in 1950, and its ranks grew to over 4000 sisters in more than 100 countries. These sisters take the three traditional vows of chastity, poverty and obedience, and add to it a fourth: To give wholehearted free service to the poorest of the poor.

FAITH AND THE LIFE OF JOY

When you are helping thousands who have nothing, the work never ends. So imagine how exhausting her work must have been, particularly when her health began to fail. She had a heart attack when she was seventy-three. Events like these are often followed by changes in lifestyle. People tend to dial it back a notch and start to take things easier, particularly at her age, but not Mother Teresa.

Her second heart attack came when she was seventy-nine. That setback was also too small to get her to retire. She led the Missionaries of Charity until she was eighty-six years old before retiring. She died six months later. No one was forcing her to work until a few months before her death. But unlike many workaholics, I cannot imagine her having any regrets on her death bed regarding the amount of time she spent working.

Her passion for her work illustrates one of the greatest blessings of the Path to Christlikeness. We are given assignments that engage our spiritual gifts and this not only ensures our fruitfulness, it also makes our work enjoyable. It is inherently pleasurable to exercise our giftedness and Mother Teresa's life illustrates this truth.

RECEIVING THE VISION

The trumpet of God that calls us to action is typically silent to the rest of the world. Pierce did not see a "vision"—the heavens failed to open up—nor did he hear the voice of God or of angels. Instead, a battered little girl enabled him to see what God wanted him to see.

Mother Teresa's heart was prepared for her "call within the call" by the omnipresent poverty she began to see in a different light. Her eyes of faith saw an unmet need and it stirred something deep inside of her.

Sometimes our assignment leads us into the dark wilderness of the righteous, as it appears to have done to both Pierce and Mother Teresa, but we do not remain in it. After the Day of Atonement comes the seventh and final feast that is called by several names: Ingathering, Booths and Tabernacles. It was to be a joyous occasion.

> You shall *rejoice* in your feast ...because the LORD your *God will bless you* in all your produce and in all the work of your hands, so that *you will be altogether joyful* (Dt 16:14, 15, emphasis added).

This festival is what the wilderness of the righteous prepares us for: The spiritual joy of celebrating with God. It is a foretaste of heaven.

THE SPIRITUAL FRUIT OF HOPE

THE PRINCE OF PREACHERS

Charles Haddon Spurgeon did not live a long life. He died at the age of fifty-seven, but his years were productive. He published seventy-five volumes of sermons, and the 3,500 sermons he delivered were sometimes given at a pace of ten per week. He wrote over 135 books and edited another twenty-eight.

One reason why he was so productive as a pastor was his early start. When he was nineteen years old (!), he received the call to be the pastor of one of the largest Baptist congregations in London, the New Park Street Chapel. Within a matter of months, the congregation had outgrown the chapel and Spurgeon was speaking to crowds numbering 10,000 people.

Could such heady success for a young man make him conceited? According to his own writings it at least threatened to do so, and how could it not? To prevent this, Christ gave him a "thorn in the flesh" so that he would turn to Jesus for grace for the remainder of his days.

SPURGEON'S THORN

He was only twenty-two years old when he was preaching a sermon to a crowd of 10,000, at the Surrey Gardens Music Hall. Thousands more waited outside, jamming the exits, hoping to get in. Then someone yelled fire and in the panic that followed several people were trampled to death. Spurgeon was devastated by this and sank into a deep depression that he never fully recovered from.

His life-long battle with depression would leave him bedridden for days and even weeks. He felt so guilty about his absences that he considered leaving the pulpit. But his church persuaded him that it was better to have him less frequently than never at all.

Spurgeon spoke openly about his struggles with depression and wondered if it was to be expected when laboring for the Lord:

> Our work, when earnestly undertaken, lays us open to attacks in the direction of depression. Who can bear the weight of souls without sinking to the dust? Passionate longings after men's conversion, if not fully satisfied (and when are they?) consume the soul with anxiety and disappointment. ... All mental work tends to weary and to depress, for much study is a weariness of the flesh—but ours is more than mental work—it is heart work, the labour of our inmost soul. How often, on the Lord's evenings, do we feel as if life were completely washed out of us! ...It is our duty and our privilege to exhaust our lives for Jesus.[3]

OUR LIFE LINE OF HOPE

What was it that sustained Spurgeon as he carried his cross daily? It was the same hope that can support us. I am reminded of Luther's words, "By faith we begin, by hope we continue." It puts the upsets of this life into an eternal perspective by focusing on heaven's distant shore. Spurgeon wrote:

> Could a man live without hope? Men manage to survive the worst condition of distress when they are encouraged by a hope....
>
> The swimmer who is ready to sink, if he sees a boat nearing him, plucks up his courage and swims with all his strength,

---

[3] Charles Haddon Spurgeon, *Lectures to My Students: A Selection of Addresses Delivered to the Students of the Pastor's College, Metropolitan Tabernacle* (London: Passmore and Alabaster, Paternoster Buildings, 1875), p. 170.

because now he expects that his swimming will be of effectual service to him. The Christian amid the waves and billows of adversity retains his hope, a glorious hope of future bliss, and therefore he strikes out like a man towards the heavenly shore. Our hope buoys up the soul, keeps the head above water, inspires confidence, and sustains courage.[4]

Spurgeon knew that suffering depression was his personal thorn, his unique wilderness, but its negative impact was balanced by the hope of a blessing that typically followed:

Depression comes over me whenever the Lord is preparing a larger blessing for my ministry. Depression has now come to me a prophet in rough clothing—a John the Baptist heralding the nearer coming of my Lord's richer blessing.[5]

The cross of Christ is never punishment for a believer. Its goal is to prepare us for God's blessing that we might serve Him more fruitfully. Spurgeon believed that those who served in the public eye were particularly in need of continual humbling. Or as he put it:

The man shall be emptied of self, and then filled with the Holy Spirit. … Uninterrupted success and unfading joy in it would be more than our weak heads could bear. Our wine needs to be mixed with water, lest it turn our brains. My witness is, that those who are honoured of their Lord in public, have usually to endure a secret chastening, or to carry a peculiar cross, lest by any means they exalt themselves, and fall into the snare of the devil.

The lesson of wisdom is *be not dismayed by soul-trouble.* …Should the power of depression be more than ordinary, think not that all is over with your usefulness. …Even if the enemy's foot be on your neck, expect to rise and overthrow him.[6]

Spurgeon understood the purpose of the cross, how we are emptied of self in order to be filled with the Holy Spirit, and with this filling comes great joy. But he also knew that "uninterrupted success and unfading joy" might eventually lead him down Satan's path of self-exaltation. It would place Jesus at the margins of his life instead of at its center. Therefore, to protect

---

[4] C. H. Spurgeon, *The Metropolitan Tabernacle Pulpit: Sermons Preached and Revised, v. XVI* (London: Passmore and Alabaster: 1871), p. 486.
[5] Quoted in H. L. Wayland, *Charles Spurgeon: His Faith and Works* (Philadelphia: American Baptist Publication Society, 1892), p. 127.
[6] Charles Haddon Spurgeon, *Lectures to My Students,* p. 178.

His faithful servant, Jesus gave Spurgeon a thorn that forced him to turn to Him for grace for the rest of his life.

There is a seasonal rhythm to the Path. Periods of fruitfulness are followed by periods of pruning. These ups and downs of the Path can be disorienting until we understand they are God's way of protecting us from becoming conceited so that He can bless us yet again.

THE FINAL FEAST: FRUITFULNESS AND JOY

We've seen how the Apostle Peter was repeatedly filled with the Holy Spirit, and the same can be said about the Apostle Paul. When Ananias met Paul, he told him that he was sent by Jesus so that he might see again and be filled with the Holy Spirit (see Ac 9:17). Later we read that when Paul met Elymas, a sorcerer, he was "filled with the Holy Spirit" (Ac 13:9). Later still, while on an evangelistic journey with Barnabas, Paul and "the disciples were filled with *joy and the Holy Spirit*" (Ac 13:52, emphasis added).

Joy is the promise of the seventh feast, Ingathering, and of the Path. It comes from being filled with God's Spirit. The wilderness is not our home. It is more like a boot camp that breaks down our fallen nature so that we might be built back up into Christ's likeness.

Hope and joy are gifts of God that often accompany one another. The Spirit of God pours both of them into our lives, and we see these disparate strands intertwining in Paul's benediction:

> May the God of *hope* fill you with all *joy* and peace in believing, so that by the power of the Holy Spirit you may *abound in hope* (Rom 15:13, emphasis added).

To abound in hope is to have a surplus, or more than enough. It is to overflow with hope. When the Infinite is poured into the finite container of our flesh, we cannot help but overflow. We freely receive God's grace that we might freely give.

Faith and hope express the beauty of God, but they are not the crowning expression of the Christian life. That honor goes to love. For "God is love" (1 Jn 4:8), and if we are to become Christlike, then we must express this love.

THE SPIRITUAL FRUIT OF LOVE

BEARING THE FRUIT OF LOVE IN THE WILDERNESS

It was a night he would never forget. After North Korea's communist army invaded South Korea, soldiers awakened the family of Joon Gon

Kim and marched them to the top of a mountain to kill them. Murdering others was celebrated as a manifestation of one's revolutionary spirit. After extensive blows to the head, Kim's father fell down dead in front of him. Next came his wife. She told Kim good-bye, and that she would meet him in heaven, before they savagely beat her to death.

Now it was his turn. The insurgents beat him until he collapsed. Then consciousness returned. They saw this, and his beating resumed. Finally, when consciousness again returned, he found himself alone.

He rushed back home and found his daughter was still alive. They fled to hide in caves, but he was discovered and again condemned to die. On one occasion his throat would have been cut were it not for a woman's protests. She did not want his blood soiling her floor.

After this, his communist persecutors planned to tie him up in a sack and toss him into the sea, but they were called away on an urgent mission at the last moment. Eventually 2,000 of the island's inhabitants were murdered.

He knew little peace during this time, until he remembered his Savior, Jesus. By renewing his fellowship with the Lord he obtained a peace that surpasses the world's understanding. He also began to view his fear as a sin, confessed it, and found himself armed with a supernatural courage and love. Love, one of our mightiest weapons, was then wielded by Kim in an overpowering way.

With his daughter in tow, he went to visit the home of one of the murderers of his wife and father. He did not go to chastise or shame this person, but to share the gospel of salvation. This is what the love of God looks like. His love can be expressed even to the murderers of one's family, so that they might be liberated from Satan's prison and transformed into powerful servants of God.

The gospel "is the power of God for salvation to everyone who believes..." (Ro 1:16). It can save the worst people, and this ruthless murderer was no match for it. He began to weep as he heard about Christ and later became a powerful witness among the communists. If you want to win in the battle against Satan, then free his slaves.

After the war ended, Kim traveled to the U.S. to study theology and deepen his understanding of the faith. While there, he was introduced to Bill Bright who asked him to join the staff of Campus Crusade and start their work in South Korea. He joined them and the results were not long in coming.

Kim evangelized Korean college students, but his impact extended far beyond the university setting. He became a shaper of the South Korean church. His evangelistic training conference, EXPLO '74, hosted 329,419 delegates. And between 1 and 1.5 million people attended each of the five evening meetings. This success was surpassed by his 1980 conference entitled, *Here's Life South Korea.* Ten million attended and 1.3 million accepted Christ as their Savior.

The impact of Kim on the spiritual life of South Korea was immense, but could he have been so richly blessed by God if he had not first gone through the wilderness of the righteous? Would he have been able to express the love of Christ to the murderer of his wife and father, if he had not experienced the cross and understood the depth of Christ's love?

Probably not.

BILL BRIGHT

Bill Bright was a successful businessman whose business was making candy. As his business grew, so did his commitment to Jesus. He felt the call to leave the business world to study theology and did so. He was months away from graduating when he felt called again to share the good news throughout the world starting with college students. He left school prior to graduation and started Campus Crusade for Christ. I imagine that in the eyes of God, he had learned all the theology he needed.

Campus Crusade started its work at UCLA and this resulted in 250 students claiming Jesus as their Savior. It spread to other campuses across the U.S. and overseas to South Korea, as we've just seen.

In 1979, Campus Crusade produced the Jesus Film, one of the most successful and widely used evangelistic tools ever made. It depicts the life of Jesus as told in the Gospel According to Luke, and was translated into over 200 languages. According to the website www.Jesusfilm.org, this film has led over 200 million people to a saving faith in Jesus.

Even if these numbers are wildly exaggerated, and the number of people who were led to a saving faith was *merely* 20,000,000, the impact of this film would still be staggering.

A self-sacrificing love for others led Bright to leave his business and his seminary training to make an outsized impact on millions of others. He is an illustration of the love symbolized by the cross. The cross empties us of self to the point where we can sacrifice our lives for others—to the degree that our circumstances allow—just as Jesus did for us on the cross.

We may not be led to leave everything to serve Jesus full time. To do this, unless led by the Spirit, might lead to frustration and futility. But as we run our candy-making business, or do whatever it is we do, our expression of Jesus' love can transform the lives of those around us.

HARD HEARTS MELT BEFORE GOD'S LOVE

In Charles Colson's book, *The Body*, he tells the story of his interview with an aggressive reporter from PBS who made it quite clear to him that she was no member of his church. She "grilled" him about his "religious experience," her description of his conversion to Christ.

The interview then covered one of the worst times of Colson's life. He was in prison and was unable to attend his father's funeral:

> Then my teenage son got into trouble. I anguished over him, desperate to help, but there I was—locked in prison, helpless. It was the lowest point in my life.
>
> It was then that my friend and brother in Christ, Al Quie, called me in prison. He had found an old statute that would allow me to go free—if someone else came to serve the rest of my prison sentence. Al, at the time the sixth-ranking Republican member of Congress, offered to take my place in prison so I could go help my son.
>
> As I told that story, the reporter's eyes filled with tears. She ordered the camera crew to stop filming and excused herself to repair her makeup. Moments later she returned, and with an air of confidence, resumed. But it was no use. The tears flowed again, and this time she paid them no attention.
>
> The power of love cannot be resisted.[7]

Yes, fruitful Christians spend long hours in the wilderness bearing their cross—in the case of Colson, his wilderness was prison—but this increases their understanding of Christ's love as expressed by His crucifixion. Then, as this understanding enables them to be "filled with all the fullness of God," they are empowered by the Holy Spirit to love with Christ's self-sacrificing love.

When we understand Christ's love it is like seeing Him for the first time, as He is, and "we know that *when he appears we shall be like him, because we shall see him as he is*" (1 Jn 3:2, emphasis added). Understanding the love of Christ leads to Christlikeness.

This ability to love others with the love of Christ comes from the Holy Spirit. The empty space at the center of our souls is initially filled with our ambitious longings, our desire to exalt ourselves, and this diseased condition is removed by the cross to make room for the love of Christ:

> ...God's love has been poured into our hearts through the Holy Spirit who has been given to us (Ro 5:5).

Our love for God and others does not originate in our hearts. We are the recipients of God's love, His unmerited favor, and upon it we both depend

---

[7] Charles Colson with Ellen Santilli Vaughan, *The Body* (Dallas, Texas: Word Publishing, 1996), p. xx.

and thrive. For grace is the power of God that enters His servants and overflows the banks of their being. We share this love from God by word and deed, and by this we free the spiritually enslaved among us, and also nourish the spiritually-famished children of God as they carry their cross through the wilderness. Our love toward our brothers and sisters in Christ can sometimes be the cup of cold water that enables their parched soul to continue until they are fully refreshed by the Spirit of God.

BIBLICAL PATTERNS

The Bible is full of hidden patterns. The seven feasts of Moses, for example, follow the 1 – 4 – 7 pattern that first appears in the seven days of the Creation Week.

On the *first* day "God said, 'Let there be light,' and there was light" (Gn 1:3). The next two days prepared the earth for habitation. On the *fourth* day there was a different operation of "light." "God said, 'Let there be lights'…" (Gn 1:14), and the next two days were spent inhabiting the earth. This movement achieved its culmination in the *seventh* day of rest.

In like manner the *first* feast, Passover, set in motion God's great plan of salvation. His children are saved by faith in the blood of the Lamb of God and are indwelt by the Holy Spirit. And then during the *fourth* feast, Pentecost, there is a different operation of the Holy Spirit. The person who was saved by faith, is now filled with the Holy Spirit. This divine anointing achieves its fulfillment during the *seventh* feast, the final harvest of spiritual fruit.

This 1 – 4 – 7 pattern is not accidental. It is repeated throughout Scripture and history. If you want to see how God's sacred history (His plan of salvation and the fulfillment of His prophecies) conforms to this pattern, then please visit http://www.tompayne.com/the-architecture-of-time.html. It reveals how the many time patterns scattered throughout the Bible are like puzzle pieces that, when put together, reveal the contours of time. What is remarkable is the way God's sacred history follows these contours.

There is a symmetry to history that is beautiful and I hope you will explore it. It will fortify your faith in a sovereign God, for only God could control the countless variables of history and make them conform to a time pattern. This faith in a sovereign God in turn will help enable you to rest, confident that the chaos we see is an illusion, for God is in control.

Finally, loving God and others, with God's love, is the definition of Christlikeness, and when we reach this level of spiritual maturity we will now be resting in Jesus, the conclusion of our restless quest.

CONCLUSION: REST

THE MYSTERY OF REST

We have now arrived at the pinnacle of spiritual achievement on the Path to Christlikeness: Rest. It is the blessed and holy capstone of creation:

> So God blessed the seventh day and made it holy, because on it God *rested* from all his work that he had done in creation (Gen 2:3, emphasis added).

The above verse contributes to our understanding of the mystery of "rest." In it the word "rested," or "shabath," could be translated *cease,* or *ceased.*[1] A translation of the above verse could read: "So God blessed the seventh day and made it holy, because on it God *ceased* from all his work that he had done in creation." To *stop* working was holy, and to *cease* working was rest. Here is why.

THE RELATIONSHIP OF REST AND WORK

When Jesus asks us to come to Him for rest it is, upon closer inspection, a most unusual offer:

> Come to me, *all who labor* and are heavy laden, and *I will give you rest. Take my yoke upon you*, and learn from me, for I am gentle and lowly in heart, *and you will find rest for your souls.* For my yoke is easy, and my burden is light (Mt 11:28-30, emphasis added).

His offer of rest is strange because it comes with a yoke, a work tool. A yoke enables two oxen to work side-by-side and pull the same load, like a

---

[1] The word "shabath" is translated "cease," "ceased," "ceases," "put a stop," "put an end," "stop," and "stopped" forty times. It is translated "rest," and "rested" six times.

plow or a cart. While one ox is very strong, two oxen, yoked together, are much stronger.

In this world of divine inversion, we are to find rest through working, though it is by working in a different way. By donning Jesus' yoke, and working by His side, we rest, or cease working, because it is God who is performing the work. This is why His "yoke is easy," and donning it enables us to rest (or cease working) and, at the same time, be fruitful and productive. The branch is fruitful, but only if the branch *rests* in the vine so that it can be supplied with grace, the unmerited power of God.

Being taught, or discipled, by Jesus is also tied to our achieving rest. Jesus tells us, "learn from me," and the American Standard Version translates this "learn of me." This is followed by: "for I am gentle and lowly in heart, and you will find rest for your souls."

To "learn of Jesus" is to learn about humility, or lowliness of heart. It is to experience the humbling wilderness and the cross. It is a way of saying, "Until you are humbled, emptied of self, you cannot rest."

Finally, let us look at what is called an "unequal yoking." A lamb being yoked to an ox is an unequal yoking because of the size and strength difference between the two animals. Wherever the much larger and stronger ox chooses to go, the smaller, weaker lamb must follow.

The Bible tells us we are not to be unequally yoked to people, but if we are to end our restless quest, then we must be unequally yoked to Jesus. When we are yoked to the Almighty Son of God we go where He goes, and become an image of His grace to the world.

SABBATH WORK AND REST

Working on the Sabbath violated God's law, yet Jesus did the healing work of a physician on this day. Since Jesus was without sin, His healing work must either redefine "work," or the "Sabbath," or both.

After Jesus healed an invalid by the Bethesda pool on the Sabbath, the Jews protested. Jesus told them that God is always working, as was He. And then He added:

> Truly, truly, I say to you, the Son can do nothing of his own accord, but only what he sees the Father doing (Jn 5:19).

Jesus had ceased working so that the Father might work in and through Him. Jesus, the image of God, was not working, because images do not work. For example, imagine a person working in front of a mirror. The person is the one doing the work, while the image reflects this work for others to see. This is the role Jesus played. He saw what the Father was doing and reflected this activity on earth.

Jesus' submission to the Father was modeling how we are to be images of God, reflecting Christ and expressing His power. We walk alongside of Him because we are yoked to Him, but it is the Son of God who is doing the work. The natural—our work—gives way to the supernatural—Christ's work—as we cease working and express Christ's power. This is the essence of both rest and Christlikeness.

GOD'S SOVEREIGNTY AND REST

According to Jesus our ability to rest, free from anxiety, should come from a deep-rooted belief in God's sovereignty. Jesus appeals to this sovereignty when He tells us to stop worrying about tomorrow, because God governs the remotest corners of creation, even the world of plants:

> And why are you anxious about clothing? Consider the lilies of the field, how they grow: *they neither toil nor spin*, yet I tell you, even Solomon in all his glory was not arrayed like one of these. But if God so clothes the grass of the field, which today is alive and tomorrow is thrown into the oven, will he not much more clothe you, O you of little faith? (Mt 6:28-30, emphasis added).

Note how the flower has ceased working (it neither toils nor spins), and yet is gloriously clothed. Our life's work is faith (Jn 6:29), and that is another way of saying, our life's work is resting. For, according to Martin Luther, "…faith is denial of ourselves, total rejection of self and reliance on God's grace." Self-denial and relying on the power of Christ (God's grace) is the same thing as being unequally yoked to the Son of God so that He is the one pulling the plow. This is rest and this is faith. In the world of divine inversions, our life's work is to rest.

If God was not sovereign over history, then the Word of God would be incoherent. For His sovereignty is required to fulfill the promise that all things work together for the good of those who love God (Rom 8:28). If *all things* work together for the good, then *all things* are controlled by a sovereign God. Chance cannot order good outcomes for anyone.

WAITING, ABIDING, RESTING

The timing of God can be frustrating, but if we cannot wait patiently for the realization of His plan for our lives, then we cannot rest. God, in His wisdom, makes us wait, and these delays that plague our old nature become one of life's most effective faith tests. It is designed to produce steadfastness, patience, and the ability to wait without complaint or concern. We underestimate the value of this, but God does not:

> Count it all joy, my brothers, when you meet trials of various kinds, for you know that the *testing of your faith* produces

steadfastness. And let steadfastness have its full effect, that *you may be perfect and complete, lacking in nothing* (Jm 1:2-4, emphasis added).

Paul's life illustrates this spiritual principle. He was forced to wait in prison on several occasions, and as he waited time was wasting away. Or was it? What if time can be invested in eternity? In prison he wrote three of his most spiritually profound epistles (Ephesians, Philippians and Colossians), receiving and capturing for us the eternal Word of God.

Time is irrelevant when it comes to an eternal God fulfilling His will. The Apostle Paul went on only four missionary journeys, that we know of, and wrote thirteen letters. This took little time, and yet his work changed the trajectory of human history. For it does not matter how long or hard we work, or how much we produce, but how Christ anoints our work. Jesus can accomplish in seconds what centuries of hard work cannot achieve.

THE SECRET OF THE CHRISTIAN LIFE

I return to Watchman Nee's book, *Sit, Walk, Stand,* that God used to save me. It tells us that resting in Christ is the Christian Path to power:

> What is the secret strength of the Christian life? Whence has its power? Let me give you the answer in a sentence: *The Christian's secret is his rest in Christ.* His power derives from his God-given position. All who sit can walk, for in the thought of God the one follows the other spontaneously. We sit forever with Christ that we may walk continuously before men. Forsake for a moment *our place of rest in him,* and immediately we are tripped and our testimony in the world is marred, but abide in Christ, and our position there ensures the power to walk worthy of him here. If you desire an illustration of this kind of progress, think, first of all, not of a runner in a race but of a man in a car, or better still, of a cripple in a power driven invalid carriage. What does he do? He goes—but he also sits.[2]

WILDERNESS OR REST?

We know the Israelites were condemned to wandering in the wilderness until they died there, but God added this, which pertains to rest:

> For forty years I loathed that generation
> and said, "They are a people who go astray in their heart,
> and *they have not known my ways.*"

---

[2] Watchman Nee, pp. 34-35, emphasis added.

> Therefore I swore in my wrath,
> "They *shall not enter my rest*" (Ps 95:10-11, emphasis added).

As the author of Hebrews meditated on these verses he concluded, "So we see that they were unable to enter because of unbelief" (Heb 3:19). In other words, their lack of faith made it impossible to enter the Lord's rest. But the above verses also add, "they have not known my ways."

To be at peace while we walk the Path is difficult when we do not understand God's "ways." When His "ways" make no sense to us, we are perplexed and disturbed. This book is an attempt to remedy that shortcoming by revealing the signposts—the seven feasts of Moses—that mark the Path to Christlikeness. They show how our faith will constantly be tested by fire, purifying it to the point where we stop turning to self, and only turn to Jesus. When we reach this point, we rest.

Faith attaches us to the vine from which flows Christ's Spirit, and it enables us to love others as He loved us. Jesus said, "just as I have loved you, you also are to love one another. By this all people will know that you are my disciples, if you have love for one another" (Jn 13:34-35). The disciples of Jesus are identified by their Christlike love for one another, for it makes them images of the Image of God. When we naturally express this love the operations on our heart are over. In this world of divine inversions, we've been turned inside-out, reversing the effects of the Fall.

It is our resting in Jesus that ends our restless quest. He gives our lives meaning. There is no fruitless toil for the branch abiding in the vine. Completion, satisfaction and rest is the lot of those who are descended from Jesus, the last Adam. He fills our emptiness with Himself, and He is the only One capable of filling this emptiness. As St. Augustine so beautifully wrote, "Thou has formed us for Thyself, and our hearts are restless till they find rest in Thee."

THE FEAST OF BOOTHS: THE END

Ingathering, the seventh and final feast, was also called the Feast of Booths, or Tabernacles. A booth was a temporary dwelling, and as such it is a metaphor of our bodies, our temporary dwelling of flesh. The ultimate end of the Christian life is to depart from our tabernacle of flesh, be clothed with an imperishable body, and be with the Father, the Son, and the Holy Spirit forever. It will open to us a world of eternal delight.

My closing prayer is that we all take courage, keep the faith, hold on to our hope of heaven and love one another as Christ loves us. Amen.